Vital Signs
Writings on Gesture

Melissa Gordon

Occasional Papers   Frans Masereel Centrum

Colour Code

Red: Contextual description of original delivery

Blue: Talking to myself

Dark Blue: Reportage voice

Green: Quotes of others

Purple: An alter ego that questions everything

Orange: Voice of my correspondents

Cyan: Repeating myself

Magenta: Me yelling

Grey: Stage instructions

Presence and Absence

(This text was delivered as a talk at Artists Space in New York, on 1 October 2015. It was part of the project "WE (Not I)," which was co-organised by Melissa Gordon and Marina Vishmidt. "WE (Not I)" was a collective editing exercise, and brought over 100 artists, writers and designers together in London and New York for two week-long residencies and public programmes. Presence and Absence was later published in May Revue 16, which was guest-edited by artist Fulvia Carnevale in 2016.)

> Increasingly as an artist, I have begun to feel that my voice is becoming disembodied from myself. Who is it that is "speaking"? It is strange to envision oneself as a construct, a concept, outside of one's own body, but that is the form perceived by others: an accumulation of objects, made by a non-entity with a vague persona, skewed and squared by gestures and contexts.

The intangible figure of the dropout speaks to this feeling of externalisation. The dropout is like a centrifugal force spinning into a spiral questions about power and relations between art objects, makers and lookers. The gesture of dropping out causes a whirlpool of escaping possibilities. In this sense, the dropout is the perfect cipher through which to view the role of the artist: the dropout deals in moves, gestures and the value at stake in these. As a character, the dropout acts outside the bounds of the playing field of contemporary art, and by doing so, reveals the edge of the field at any time.

"Dropping out" as a term could point to two specific histories: the psychedelic-driven spiritual phrase coined by psychologist Timothy Leary in 1966, "Turn on, tune in, drop out", or the condition of leaving the workforce, mid-career, as befalls many women, including many women artists. If dropping out could be thought of as a precondition for being a woman artist, let's say, during the time just preceding conceptual artist Lee Lozano's famous *Dropout Piece* (begun c.1970), then perhaps we can understand her gesture of dropping out as a biting critique of both Leary's slogan *and* of what was expected of her as a female artist. If we look more closely at the historic impulses of this action of leaving, I think we will see that the current and ongoing ramifications of dropping out in the art world, specifically for women artists, are more pointed and far-reaching.

The document that piqued my interest in the character of the dropout is the essay "Towards a Metalanguage of Evil" (1992), artist Cady Noland's entry in the Documenta IX catalogue, which accompanied her contribution to Documenta IX in Kassel the same year. In trying to decipher the motivations of the essay, one uncovers a text attempting, I believe, to make a powerful critique of the art world and art market, shortly pre-dating the discourse around institutional critique and globalisation. The text stakes out extreme positions on cause and effect, which are explored through the role-play of a psychopathic relationship. Noland begins her essay by stating that there is a "meta-game available for use in the United States. The rules of the game, or even that there is a game at all, are hidden to some."[1] She goes on to describe in an oblique manner a relationship between X and Y, in which X is constantly, in a Tom and Jerry-like scenario, trying to con Y:

> *The game is a machine composed of interconnected mechanistic devices ... A con or a snow job is the site at which X preys upon the hopes, fears, anxieties of Y for ulterior motives and/or personal gain ... These machinations exist a priori of X and Y as an indifferent set of tools and could conceivably be picked up by anyone and used against anyone else.*[2]

1   Cady Noland, "Towards a Metalanguage of Evil", *Documenta IX* (Stuttgart: Edition Cantz, 1992), 410.

2   Ibid.

began once again.

practising to be like water...

Noland sets out the essay as a game or a device. It is key, then, to regard it not as a reading of a situation or a metaphor, but purely as a theoretical overview of potential moves or gestures. It considers actions that one (an artist?) can take within a larger psychotic field (the art world?).

"Towards a Metalanguage of Evil" was first delivered as a lecture in 1987 at an academic conference called "The Expression of Evil" at West Georgia College. It was used to construct Noland's Documenta IX installation, a constellation of art objects by her peer group, including Steven Parrino, Barbara Kruger, and Sherrie Levine, circling a sculptural installation of a crashed car, and interspersed with news photos of disasters such as plane wrecks. The essay is accompanied by similar images. Interestingly, Noland begins her series of examples of moves by using the image adjustment of tabloid culture as an example of the tactics of "the game":

> *"Tabloids already use many of the game's tactics by foreshortening and "cropping" celebrities, blowing them up, and, in the case of National Enquirer television commercials, reducing them to photo-objects and then animating these objects."*[3]

Later in her essay, Noland references the film *Blow-Up* (1966) by Michelangelo Antonioni, noting that it is "through the exhumation of photographic images or audio recordings, and their repeated screening that Y searches for the telling detail (of X's 'machinations and his attempts at putting forth a bankrupt reality')."[4] There's an underlying interest in the role and performance of images in the text, and the image's relationship to capital.

Information gathering is seen throughout the essay as a way for X to win "the game", to garner a context into which X can entrap Y. Noland envisions a dystopic version of our current culture in which our online devices and apps deliver a constant stream of revenue-generating data to corporations for their capital gain. But who is the psychopath in Noland's text, which pre-dates these concerns by over a decade? Perhaps it is the drive of investment capitalism itself, as something inherent in the field of "the game" she is describing:

> *"The psychopath shares the societally sanctioned characteristics of the entrepreneurial male."*[4]

The quotes above make me question their context: what was Noland reacting to, in art history? What move was she trying to make? Her references return multiple times to the use-value of pictures and information, and how they construct ways to move or act. The artists she exhibited in her installation at Documenta IX are associated with the Pictures Generation, a group of artists who regarded single images as something that enacted a larger (often unseen) timeline, such as the series *Film Stills* (1977–80) by Cindy Sherman. The artists who Noland gathered around her in 1992 were dealing with the effect of the image in a larger sociopolitical realm. In her essay and exhibition, Noland was attempting to envision how the recontextualisation of pictures as a gesture by artists opens up a game centred around the formation of belief and value through manipulation of imagery, as a parallel to how they are used in corporate structures.

In his essay "Pictures", published in the catalogue of the eponymous exhibition at Artist Space in 1977 and then *October* magazine, curator Douglas Crimp uses both theatricality and staging as a means to differentiate the emergent "Pictures" artists from performative art practices of the 1970s in which "you had to be there". He describes the means by which Jack Goldstein, Sherrie Levine and Cindy Sherman's pictures *enact* as well as present:

3   Ibid.
4   Ibid, 412.

"The temporality of these pictures is not, then, a function of the nature of the medium as in itself temporal, but of the manner in which the picture is presented; it can obtain in a still picture as well as a moving one."[5]

So, if the precursor to enacting images in a temporal manner is a literal, performance-based staging of the image, it can be implied that there is both a frontstage and a backstage to imagery. Noland also references sociologist Erving Goffman, who in his book *The Presentation of Everyday Self* (1959), focuses on the way in which everyday actions have a backstage, often concealed from others. The hidden motivations of images, Noland suggests, gives them an autonomy that, like in horror movies, embeds something mute, dead or immobile with terrifying animation.

"Towards a Meta-Language of Evil" ends with a rumination on "waiting for reconfiguration" as a strategy akin to using shock therapy on a psychiatric patient. Noland talks about waiting for the environment in which the game is situated to change the "luck of the shuffle", as she calls it, as the last option of the psychopath. I think of it as X consciously going into hibernation in order to wait for better circumstances, or playing a long game because it is the only available option.

"If X is a psychopath, the one certain thing is that this relatively passive strategy, waiting for reconfiguration, will only be used if it is the last game in town." [6]

Noland stopped exhibiting new work in the mid-1990s and there is a veil of mystery surrounding her current presence in the form of absence. Did she set the stage for herself as an image and wait for a reshuffle, or reconfiguration, to re-emerge years later, to alter the rules of the game?

It was after reading and discussing "Towards a Metalanguage of Evil" in 2011 that I discovered in a conversation with a woman artist that Noland's work *Oozeworld* (1989) achieved the highest selling price for a work by a living woman artist (6.6 million USD at Sotheby's auction house in 2011). On 11 May 2015 her work *Bluewald* again fetched the highest price for a living woman artist – 9.8 million USD – at Christie's. It should be noted, however, that 58.4 million was the existing record sale at the time for an artwork by a living male artist.[7]

After the sale of *Oozewald* in 2011, another Noland piece titled *Cowboys Milking* (1990) was brought to auction at Sotheby's by Marc Jancou Contemporary Gallery, and Noland denied authorship of the piece, citing damage. Then, in July 2014 she disavowed the work *Log Cabin* (1990), purchased by Scott Meuller from KOW Gallery, citing inappropriate materials used for restoration, thus raising a moral dilemma around the authorship of the artist. In the denial of authorship of *Cowboys Milking* in 2011, Noland invoked the Visual Artists Rights Act of 1990, otherwise known as VARA, which states that artists hold the original moral rights to their work, regardless of ownership or copyright. In an email of 9 November 2011, sent by Noland's lawyer to Sotheby's on the evening before the scheduled auction, the artist insisted that *Cowboys Milking* (1990) was damaged and demanded that Sotheby's not sell it because "her honor and reputation [would] be prejudiced as a result of offering [it] for sale with her name associated with it".[8]

Seph Rodney's July 2015 article entitled "The Art of Cady Noland as Poison Pill," published on the online journal *Hyperallergic*, focuses on Noland's denial of the sale of *Log Cabin* (1990).[9] The article implies that Noland's action sabotages both herself and the art world and desribes her gesture as "art as bomb".[10] But in a correction, Rodney notes that what seemed originally to be a disavowal of work in the process of purchase, becomes a warning from the artist to new buyers that the current state of the work is unacceptable:

5   Douglas Crimp, *Pictures* (New York: Artists Space, 1997), 80.
6   Cady Noland, "Towards a Metalanguage of Evil", 413.
7   Jeff Koons, *Balloon Dog (Orange)*, sold on 12 November 2013 at Christie's for 58.4 million USD.
8   https://www.artnews.com/art-in-america/features/sothebys-and-jancou-battle-in-appeals-court-over-cady-noland-artwork-59382/. Last accessed 14 July 2023.
9   In the article, it is clarified that the piece being discussed is actually *Log Cabin Blank with Screw Eyes and Cafe Door (Memorial to John Caldwell)*, from 1990.
10 https://hyperallergic.com/223591/the-art-of-cady-noland-as-poison-pill/.

STACKING
HANGING
9ATHERING
INVERTING
ERASING
EXITING

"So it seems that Noland's response to the most recent buyer Meuller was essentially warning him off from believing this work was what she had crafted or intended."[11]

[OK, let's take a deep breath here.]

What initially interested me in Noland's legal battles around the question of authorship was the fact that the highest price ever paid for the work of a female artist was for one no longer present in the art world. What kind of economy is that? Further, I became interested in her legal cases as the polar opposite of those of artist Richard Prince around appropriation, in which Prince and his gallerist Larry Gagosian defend his use of other artists' imagery in his works.[12]

Instead of accumulating all voices into a meta-voice, as in Prince's practice, it is Noland's declaration of the *absence* of voice that accumulates value (and thus points to the different types of economy circulating images appropriated by these two different genders and different positions in the market). I began to think of Noland's essay "Towards a Metalanguage of Evil" as a declaration of intent akin to Lozano's *Dropout Piece* (c.1970). I began to think that absence is in general used as a strategy of valorisation of women's art practices, and that this absence is the X to the Y of presence for women artists, both historically and now. I wonder if Noland's essay provides clues to the meaning of her dropout and how this dropout relates to what I see as perhaps an attempt at a performance of a con job in the art market. Has the original – the art object – become a prop for a larger theatre of value exchange? And if so, what role is the artist playing in this production? Is it a production of denial? As with many other dropouts, Noland's gesture to leave has been used to affect both abstract and real value, and thus can also be understood as expanding the mechanism of authorship.

The question remains as to whether we can judge Noland's actions as authored moves, and if the legal language that surrounds the movement of many of her pieces, and a general lack of display and new work, is in fact an artist's voice, or simply a lawyer's voice. It also remains to be seen where the story will end: will Noland's works continue to be desirable goods? Will she help pass legislation on the earnings of artists from secondary sales, or will her work be sequestered in storerooms for years to come?

[And now, in 2023, three years after the 2020 exhibition Cady Noland at Museum für Moderne Kunst in Frankfurt, will her works exhibited there ever emerge again from their storage and private collections?]

Nevertheless, Noland is not the first artist to use dropping out as a conscious gesture, or rather, to use the presence of absence as a device. Lee Lozano, Charlotte Posenenske and Laurie Parsons, through different means, came to the same end of leaving the art world and art production because the possibilities of authorship were too narrow as an outlet for their wider practices.

I am not interested in Lozano, Posenenske or Parsons because of their obscurity. I do not believe the myths that they were "not able to hack it". Perhaps they were smart enough to wash their hands of the situation in which they found themselves, but regardless, each of their gestures expanded the role of authorship precisely because these actions existed *outside* of the playing field of art. Their acts of dropping out were simply the natural progressions of their working practices: they took their practice to the extreme of authorship and followed through.

It takes a shift in perception to consider dropping out as an act or a gesture instead of a circumstance. To do this requires the removal of an artist's biography from the understanding of their work. This is often hard when many women artists, especially

11 Ibid.
12 Donald Graham, plaintiff vs. Richard Prince, Gagosian Gallery Inc. and Lawrence Gagosian, defendants, https:// www.courthousenews.com/ wp-content/uploads/2020/07/ graham-prince-msj.pdf.

those who have exited the art world, such as painter Agnes Martin during her mental breakdown when she left New York for the New Mexico desert in the summer of 1967, are shrouded in mystique. Forgotten or undervalued female artists can encourage a sense of discovery, a cat and mouse play: the finding of hidden histories as gems that we, in the art world, are trying to uncover like truffle pigs. If we, though, consider that historically the condition of dropping out was common and expected for women artists, the conundrum of presence and absence becomes more fraught, especially in a reevaluation or revaluation of these female rarities.

From Expressionist-style works in the early 1960s, Charlotte Posenenske shifted to more sculptural and specifically machine-made artworks towards the mid-1960s, with monochrome painted aluminum sheets hung at angles on the walls. In 1967 she began her final work, *Series D* (1967/ongoing), in which a set of modular forms resembling architectural air vents can be assembled into any shape by the curator, artist, or at some point, the audience. These forms, first in cardboard and then in aluminum sheeting, are, as originally intended, sold at the cost of production in the factory where they were made. Unlike her male peers, Posenenske's modular objects were specific to their value transactions in the world – materials as form, used to create systems, ideas, not profit. As a strategy, her gesture runs in direct contradiction to her minimalist artist peers such as Carl Andre, Dan Flavin and Donald Judd, who literalised the value transformation of everyday materials, exemplifying the disembodied aura of authorship. Posenenske's authorship finds value in a more radical relationship to exchange, and has a "Drop Out" statement from 1968, titled *manifesto*:

> *The things I make are variable,*
> *as simple as possible,*
> *reproducible.*
> *They are components of a space; since they are like building elements,*
> *they can always be rearranged into new combinations or positions.*
> *Thus, they alter the space.*
> *I leave this alteration to the consumer who thereby again and anew*
> *participates in the creation.*
> *The simplicity of the basic geometric forms is beautiful and suited to demonstrate the principles*
> *of rationalized alteration.*
> *I make series because I do not want to make single pieces for individuals,*
> *in order to have elements combinable within a system,*
> *in order to make something which is repeatable, objective, and because it is economical.*
> *The series could be prototypes for mass production.*
> *Series DW (at Fischer's) is made of corrugated pasteboard which is light and cheap: a material for consumption.*
> *Often the elements or their combinations are very large in order to alter the spatial environment*
> *more thoroughly.*
> *They approximate architectural dimensions and also for this reason differ increasingly from the former gallery objects.*
> *They are less and less recognizable as "artworks."*
> *The objects should have the objective character of industrial products.*
> *They are not intended to represent anything other than what they are.*
> *The former categorization of the arts no longer exists.*
> *The artist of the future should have to work with a team of specialists in a development laboratory.*
> *Though art's formal development has progressed at an increasing tempo,*
> *its social function has regressed.*
> *Art is a product of temporary topicality, yet, the market is minute while*

It is this history of voice that I will keep in mind when I think about the question: who is speaking, in relationship to painting and its desire. Most especially, the sense of how words is connected to the projection of a painter onto a painting.

prestige and prices rise the less topical the supply is.
It is painful for me to face the fact that art cannot contribute to the solution
of urgent social problems.
Offenbach, February 11, 1968[13]

Posenenske ceased production in 1968 and retrained as a sociologist specialising in industrial working practices. She felt that art could not create social change or redress inequity, and she abandoned any participation in the art world until her death in 1985. Her works have been re-staged and enacted by others for years afterwards. Her impulse to create or effect change without authorship mirrors the practice of another artist, Laurie Parsons, whose art became so ephemeral that she moved gradually and laterally into the role of a social worker. The little I know about Parsons comes from art critic Bob Nickas's article in *Artforum* from April 2003, which begins: "An artist sends her slides to a gallery and is asked to take part in a group show. (And how often does that happen? Does never sound about right?)"[14] In 1990, Parson's show at the Lawrence Monk gallery was empty of work: "I felt it essential that I consider the gallery itself, rather than continue to unquestioningly use it as a context. With its physical space and intricate social organisation, it is as real, and as meaningful, as the artwork it houses and markets."[15] My favorite recollection by Nickas of a piece of Parsons' is of a stack of 300 single dollar bills at the New Museum, New York, with instructions to the guards not to stop audience members from taking them. What can be said of it besides: "It quickly disappears"?[16]

Parsons was contemporaneous with Rirkrit Tiravanija and Felix Gonzalez-Torres, artists whose own biographies bring powerful subjectivities and narratives into play with conceptual, sparse and often "found" objects as installations, but where is Parsons in her work, as a character? She is absent in comparison; of course, she is present, just less recognisable as author. Is she absent simply because of the lack of discourse around her work incorporating her into history? Or rather is she absent because there is no place in what we understand in art history as authorship for her gestures because her practice's natural conclusion is an opening out rather than a clarifying move? To quote Parsons: "Art must spread into other realms, into spirituality and social giving."[17] In Nickas's article from the early 2000s, he tells us that Parsons left the art world behind and became an advocate for the mentally ill in New York City.

Why couldn't these women artists remain in the art world and continue to feel they were giving? Why did they believe they had to leave to contribute something to people?

13   Charlotte Posenenske, "Statement", *Art International*, 12, no. 5 (May 68): 50.
14   Bob Nickas, "Whatever Happened To: Dematerial Girl (Laurie Parsons)", *Artforum*, vol. 41, no. 8 (April 2003).
15   Ibid.
16   Ibid.
17   Ibid.
18   Most of Lee Lozano's works that are considered "pieces" or "actions" were transferred from a notebook to an A4 page of paper. They were written by hand in capital letters. *Dropout Piece* does not have a formal "write up" on A4 paper, and thus it is questionable whether it is truly an action.
19   Sarah Lehrer-Graiwer, *Lee Lozano: Dropout Piece* (London: Afterall Books, 2014), 74

Lee Lozano is now perhaps the most widely known dropout artist, but her famous – and completely ephemeral[18] – *Dropout Piece* (begun c.1970), as with other dropout statements, was the logical conclusion of a practice based on the *living out* of instruction pieces. To quote art historian Lucy Lippard on Lozano: "Her art, it has been said, becomes the means by which to transform her life, and by implication, the lives of others and the planet itself."[19] Again, like Posenenske, Lozano puts a dark mirror up to her artistic peers: her ballpoint, handwritten, all-caps, instructional language flies in the face of the dry businesslike type-written language of her conceptualist peers. Lozano is a mythic character for many who first heard of her in the early 2000s: her story was shrouded in sadness like Posenenske's and Parsons', although the reality of all three artists' histories is more inspiring than originally told: their lives and practices were more embedded and critical to the world around them than those of most artists. Counter to the myth I first heard, that Lozano dropped out and disappeared back home to Texas, where she died of breast cancer and drug addiction, author Sarah Lehrer-Graiwer's book *Dropout Piece* (2014) uncovers the fact that Lozano was enacting *Dropout Piece* in New York for a decade: hanging out at CBGB's with musicians Joey Ramone and Patti Smith, posing, dancing, talking and participating in the persona-driven punk scene of the 1970s. She was present as absent, just undocumented. Let's read what might actually be Lozano's original *Dropout Piece*, an entry in her diary:

I HAVE NO IDENTITY
I HAVE AN APPROXIMATE MATHEMATICAL IDENTITY
(BIRTHCHART)
I HAVE SEVERAL NAMES
I WILL GIVE UP MY SEARCH FOR IDENTITY AS A DEADEND
INVESTIGATION
I WILL MAKE MYSELF EMPTY TO RECEIVE COSMIC INFO
I WILL RENOUNCE THE ARTIST'S EGO, THE SUPREME TEST
WITHOUT WHICH BATTLE A HUMAN COULD NOT BECOME
"OF KNOWLEDGE"
I WILL BE HUMAN FIRST, ARTIST SECOND
I WILL NOT SEEK FAME, PUBLICITY, OR SUCKSESS IDENTITY
CHANGES CONTINUOUSLY AS MULTIPLIED BY TIME
(IDENTITY AS VECTOR)[20]

> For all dropouts, it is the edges of themselves that dissolve *into* their work. The idea of an identity defined by the authorship of art is too narrow. Dropouts misbehave according to the rules of the game: not pursuing self-promotion but rather self-discovery. Over and over again the dropout presents a negative shape of authorship, running counter to value creation in art history. The dropout can also be situated within feminist art history: early feminist works foregrounded the personal/body/felt relationships to objects as much as authorial ones.

> Tacking left, let's think about the term "derivative value": in finance, a derivative is a contract that derives its value from the performance of an underlying asset, with which its fictional future is traded.

Art historian David Joselit, in his 2013 essay "On Aggregators" describes a possible way to understand an exit from contemporary art. Here, the "contemporary" is defined not as a time, but a thing, a situation; a situation in which we are repeating the value structures of appropriation and postmodernism endlessly. We are not original, nor do we endeavour to be:

> *One of the great impediments to an understanding of global contemporary art is the vexing problem of the derivative. From a perspective that overvalues innovation, it is difficult to credit works of art that speak in idioms invented elsewhere. But this is what much art made outside of the West, not to mention the preponderance of art made in the West, has done since around 1980, when strategies of appropriation and postmodern pastiche entered American and European art. From the perspective of an international style, the derivative is no longer a problem since what matters is not the invention of a visual idiom or style but how rhetorically effective it is in its particular utterances.*[21]

> The dropout is a negative character, but only in the sense of creating negative space in a world with so much aggregation. Taking a step back from the frontstage allows one to play with the normative role of the artist. From this stance, I can embody myself as a performer one step removed from the action: at once a painter, a director, an editor. I look to the dropout because in it I see a freedom of movement in an art world seemingly driven by authorship. As a device, dropping out is a radical thing, something with no capital value to exchange, no information to cull, just a gesture, for all that it's worth.

20 Ibid., 76.
21 David Joselit, "On Aggregators", *October*, no.146 (Fall 2013): 5.

Luxury Goods (A Burning Desire)

(Originally delivered as a spoken performance in the exhibition "The Reading Room" at Montague Space, London, on 27 September 2016.)

But when the web is pulled askew, hooked up at the edge, torn in the middle, one remembers that these webs are not spun in mid-air by incorporeal creatures, but are the work of suffering human beings, and are attached to grossly material things, like health and money and the houses we live in.[1]

Ownership is the root of all grievances. We can see this in the first code of law, an ancient Babylonian text developed solely to bring order to the exchange of goods, and to enact physical punishment to protect value. I come from a Sicilian American family, where the feeling of grievance in general falls under the much-used term *agita*, a word that translates bluntly as "heartburn", but which also applies to a general but distinctly coming-from-the-gut sense of agitation. So, one could say "The eggplant has given me *agita*," but also "Your moaning is giving me *agita*." There's also a strong sense within Italian Americans of the imagination of discomfort: so a common saying might be: "Just *thinking* about the situation with so-and-so gives me *agita*." Recently, I've been noting a certain sense of discomfort when I think about the relationship between art and luxury goods, a rising wave of heat and unease inside my stomach when I observe how an excessive amount of value has seeped like a fluid into every crack of life.

In Silicon Valley slang, we all have what's called a "burn rate", which means basically how fast you shed money. This applies to an institution and, so I guess, to an individual as well. Thinking about this in daily terms, there are things we put into motion every day in order to burn: I have to feed my body with caffeine, nourishment and alcohol, and every calorie has a price. I may relax, but I feel like I'm still burning, and in fact I am: consuming rent, energy, bandwidth, paper and landfill. As an artist, I am expected not only to succeed in supplying my own body with all this material energy, and those who rely on me, but also to miraculously produce high-end goods, with no budget, in order to be part of the conversation.

When thinking about the term "burn rate" in the context of the production of art, I re-read literary critic Fredric Jameson's 1991 book *Postmodernism*, subtitled "or The Cultural Logic of Late Capitalism". Since capitalism is the fastest moving game in town, I thought I'd look back to this moment in 1991 at the beginning of our current globalised exchange to see the architecture of a pre-digital encounter with goods and culture, which might somehow frame our current moment better.

It's a bucolic read:

What has happened is that aesthetic production today has become integrated into commodity production generally: the frantic economic urgency of producing fresh waves of ever more novel-seeming goods (from clothing to airplanes), at ever greater rates of turnover, now assigns an increasingly essential structural function and position to aesthetic innovation and experimentation.[2]

1   Virginia Woolfe, "A Room of One's Own" (London: Hogarth Press, 1929), 44.
2   Frederic Jameson, *Postmodernism, or The Cultural Logic of Late Capitalism* (Durham: Duke University Press, 1991), 4-5.

A feeling of confusion gave me a hot sensation: was there a time when an aesthetic was autonomous from an economy?

//

> I recalled, like a flashback, reading an essay by the author Gary Greenberg that my friend Angie sent me titled *"The Confidence Man"* as I pushed my twins around the park when they were merely weeks old. Round and round I went, life at its very core destroyed by sleep deprivation, squinting at a tiny iPhone screen, coincidently just metres away from the blue plaque announcing Edgar Allen Poe's residence in London, to whom the essay begins by giving credit for creating the character of "the Diddler", i.e., the confidence man – otherwise known as a con man.

The confidence man is an American character, a product of the geography of a new, financially unregulated country: he is a traveling salesman who arrives to sell what in the end turns out to be a mere fantasy.

In Greenberg's essay, he describes how the 1857 novel *The Confidence Man: His Masquerade* by Herman Melville follows the character and the structure of the diddle. In it he lists this fantastic group of characters from Melville's book, on a boat together:

> *The passenger is right about this army of diddlers, except for one detail: the many scamps among the passengers – a doctor peddling herbal remedies, along with a stock trader, an employment agent, a philosopher, a man in rags, a couple of well-dressed men, will prove in the end to be the same man, who, in his various disguises, raises wind from stem to stern, diddling passengers out of their money, their health, their dignity – and, above all, out of their trust in their own judgement.[3]*

> But the con man is not a simple thief. He is a pedlar with a concrete good: belief. In fact, all you might get from a good con is the feeling of being swept along in the fiction of the moment: belief in what turn out to be lies, but which feel good at the time. You've lost something, but you still have the fantasy you believed in. "What the Confidence Man (in all his forms) offers his marks ... in short ... is that the future is sure to be better."[4]

//

> A con man is a shapeshifter; his truth is fluid and what's on sale is a confusion of reality.

//

By sheer coincidence I've spent a lot of time in the town Jonesborough, Tennessee, which is both the oldest town in the state and the home to the world's largest storytelling festival, held annually and attracting tens of thousands of visitors to come listen to professional storytellers reciting their "tall" tales.

The word that these storytellers use to describe the unfolding of a story is "spin". To "spin" a tale is an old European term, describing the unravelling of a ball of yarn, but is now more commonly used to describe how a politician might "turn" a story to a different angle in order to see it in a new light, which is quite a sculptural understanding of a story indeed.

//

3   Gary Greenberg, "The Confidence Man, In which the possibility that psychiatry is a diddle is discussed, with particular attention to the placebo effect and the talking cure", *The Believer*, Issue 112 (Summer 2015): 26.

4   Ibid., 28.

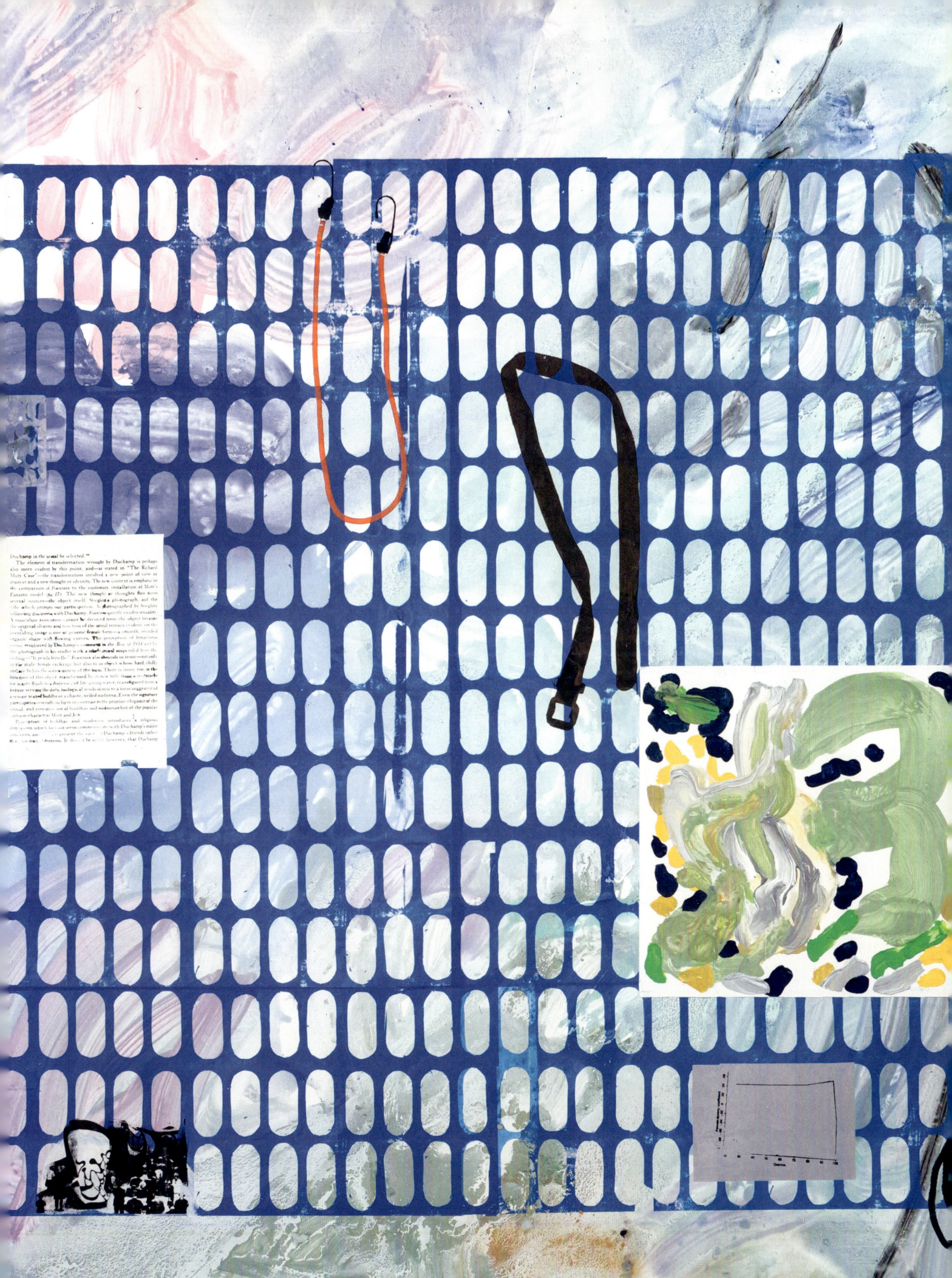

Duchamp in the *urinal* he selected.²⁰

The element of transformation wrought by Duchamp is perhaps also more evident in this piece, and so stated in "The Richard Mutt Case"—the transformation involved a new point of view in context and a new thought as to identity. The new context is emphatic in the comparison of *Fountain* to the customary installation of Mott's *Fountain* model (*fig. 17*). The new thought as thoughts flow from several sources—the object itself, its *glitzed* photograph, and the title which prompts our participation. Reinforced by his *Stieglitz* following discourse with Duchamp. *Fountain* specific exudes eroticism. A masculine association cannot be discarded from the object became the original identity and function of the urinal remains evident in the overriding image as our all *powerful* female form—a smooth, rounded organic shape with flowing contours. This perception of femininity seems reinforced by Duchamp's comment in the first of 1918 set by the photograph in his studio with a male armed wings ruled from the *etchings*, "Le peuls fens fly." *Fountain* also abounds in *traits* associated in that made female exchange but also in an object whose hard, chilly surface belies the warm waters of the womb. There is more too, in the *bling*tion of this object transformed by choice to *rely* tram a re-*readable* water flush by a *disown* of life-giving water, transfigured from a forvour serving the dirty, indelicate deeds at once to a lotus impersion of a syringe-wared Buddha or a chaste, veiled *madonna*. Even the signature pure, *spoken*—works in harm in contrast to the primitive elegance of the original, and *evocative* as of buddhas and madonnas but of the popular *tireless* character by Mutt and Jem.

Perception of buddhas and madonnas introduces a religious component which *became* even more common with Duchamp's major concerns and *associated* the *turn* to Duchamp's friends rather than his own. Numerous it does be noted, however, that Duchamp

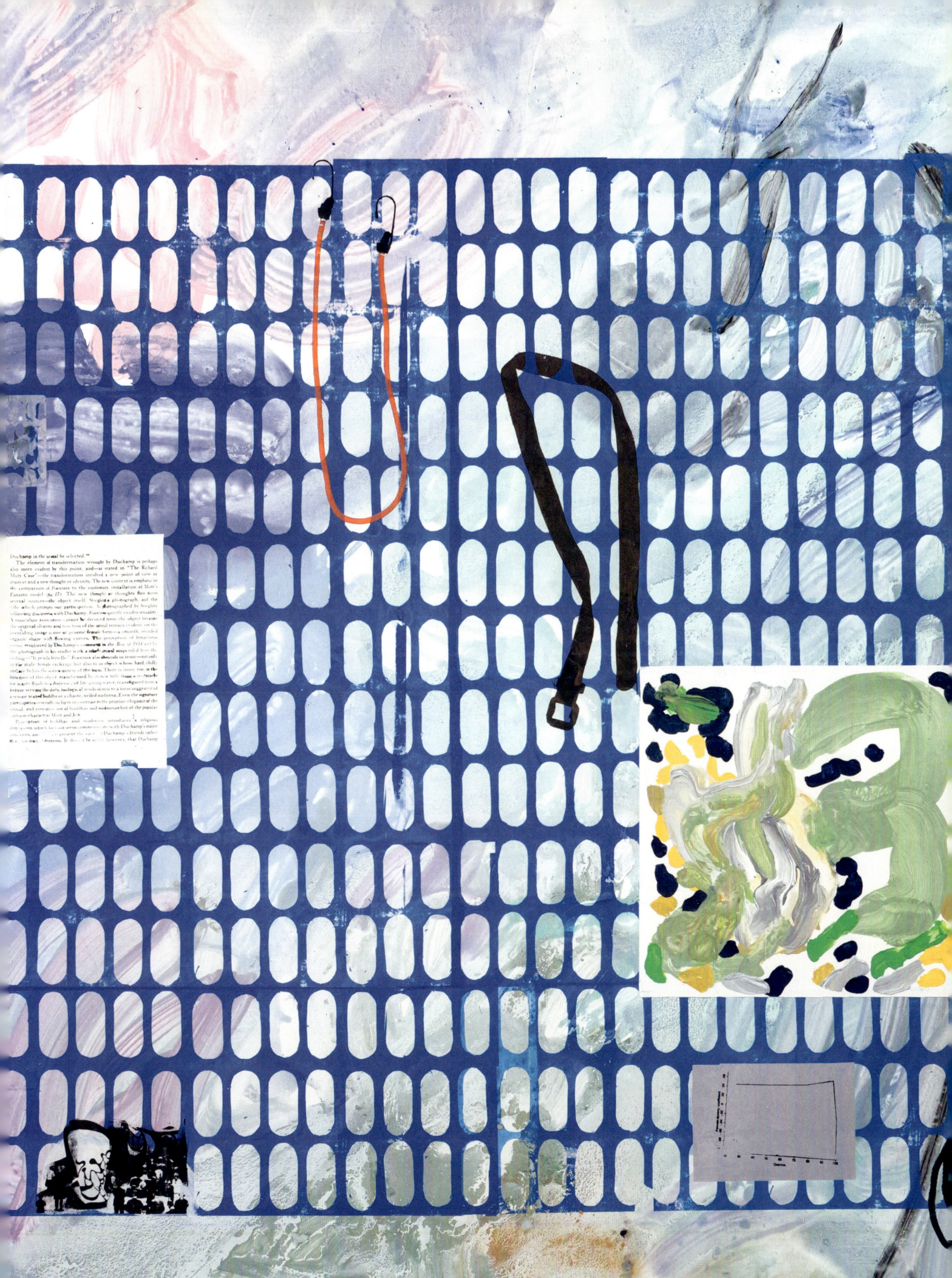

Luxury goods are items that can be thought of as unnecessary, excessive and out of reach.

If Jameson describes the postmodern as an aesthetic shape-form that reflects or contains a period of time in capitalism, specifically the period of time pre-dating a globalised, digital economy, then perhaps luxury goods can be thought of as a conduit to view a current move in the cultural field from (modernist) depth of meaning to (postmodernist) flatness of surface to the current *distance* or unattainability of all goods.

To quote Jameson:

> *But there are some other significant differences between the high modernist and the postmodernist moment ... The first and most evident is the emergence of a new kind of flatness or depthlessness, a new kind of superficiality in the most literal sense – perhaps the supreme formal feature of all the postmodernisms.*[5]

Jameson finds this difference between modernist depth and postmodernist flatness in comparing the expression of Vincent Van Gogh's *Peasant Shoes* (1888) and the expression-less surfaces of Andy Warhol's *Diamond Dust Shoes* (1980). Juxtaposing the two paintings, Jameson notes the lack of criticality, or utopic drive in Warhol's work, which he says does not in fact *speak*. I, of course, cannot but think of other glittery (shiny, full of physical labour etc.) artworks that do indeed speak only to the tight loop of value-creation.

In 2016, I would say there has been a move from postmodern flatness to a distance between us viewers and the multiple surfaces that we now encounter, often flattened through a digital screen The flat surfaces around us are out of reach, or project in their blue light an out-of-reach-ness. The distance between a burning desire and endless unattainable goods or ideas points to the creation of all aspects of our lives into luxury goods, even the most basic needs like homes, sleep, food, politics, all purchased for prices beyond what wages could ever buy. We have machines of insatiability, with endless scroll, that are never satisfied inputting into our burning bodies. A few years ago, at the height of the art-market crash, a very wealthy woman confided in me that everyone she knew, including collectors, was struggling, no matter how rich they were. And weirdly, as my stomach roiled with acid unease, I understood that she meant *what you take in is never as much as you burn.*

5   Jameson, *Postmodernism*, 4-5.

Female Genius: Vital Signs

(Originally delivered as a live reading at Kunstverein, Amsterdam on 3 March 2017, this text arises from a longer correspondence with the writer Eva Kenny, who wrote "Painting Behind Itself" on Gordon's work in 2016.)

Dear Eva, here's the text I've written for the talk tonight, which I hope outlines our discussions on our fictional Female Genius …

//

Hi Mel

Sorry my head was in such a frazz earlier when I was reading your messages in work. But if you want to read Are You a Female Genius? then yes do that …

Big kiss, peacing out for the night,

Eva xxxx

In a 2014 profile on painter Marlene Dumas in *The New York Times Magazine*, Claire Messud begins by stating: "One measure of genius is *the life force* – what Harold Bloom has dubbed, referring to Samuel Johnson, "Falstaffian vitalism."[1] Dumas is a genius, the article implies, because she has the traditional characteristics of one: vitality, energy, and Falstaffian bravado. But hers is "an exemplar of a heretofore all-but-unheralded form of genius, one specifically female. She's open, giving, relational, fluid."

Eva, what do you think, shall we begin our discussion on Female Genius with the idea of vitality? The vital signs, vitality and vitriol of Female Genius, hmm? What happens when a Female Genius gets a migraine?

Funnily enough, I sat down this morning with my second coffee and a blank Microsoft Word document, and to my right on top of the stack of books lay the yellow cover of Isabelle Graw's book *Painting Beyond Itself* (2014), which you recommended to me just as we were about to go to print with my catalogue that we named after your essay "Painting Behind Itself."[2] I think your title is funnier in terms of a correspondence with David Joselit's essay "Painting Besides Itself"(2009), but anyway …

And – look at this coincidence – Graw's essay in the book is titled "The Value of Liveliness," and it's all about vitality. Here's a quote:

This view that painting has a life of its own and can therefore "think" or "speak" is prevalent among many French historians … I would argue that we are dealing with vitalist projections here Painting is able to trigger such vitalist assumptions because of its specific language, or more precisely because of its specific indexicality … [and] once [these indexical signs] appear in the context of painting they forcefully point to the absent author who seems to be somewhat physically present in them.[3]

So, in short, a painting projects the vitality, or the life-force, of the author. But Graw also points to the longer history of liveliness and value:

1 https://www.nytimes.com/2014/08/20/t-magazine/marlene-dumas-south-african-artist-profile.html.

2 Eva Kenny, "Painting Behind Itself", in *Painting Behind Itself* (Berlin: Revolver Press, 2016), 3-11.

3 Isabelle Graw, "The Liveliness of Painting", in ibid., 79-80.

"As a topos of appraisal, liveliness has an 'astonishingly long and continued history'. The production of life and liveliness was elevated to the status of an ideal that painting and sculpture laboured to achieve well into the nineteenth century."[4]

So what do you think of this: the valuation of art focused on embodying the liveliness or likeness (mimeticism) of life, the world, nature, etc. *by* the artist (think: Caravaggio) segued in modernism into the valuation of the work of art arising from the movement of the body of the author, to project vitality? Thus the surface of an artwork *stores* the vitality of the artist's life itself.

Makes you think of the holy grail, or some myth of the fountain of youth, right? What about Joan of Arc? Was she a genius? I heard they burned her just enough for her clothes to come off and to show everyone that she was "just" a woman. Though this seems perverse, even for the English.

But YOUR title: *Painting Behind Itself* is about the absent author who remains physically present, though hidden. As I remember, you were telling me about a piece of writing you had started based on the coincidence that what is considered the first abstract painting in history consists of marks painted on top of, and obscuring, a female figure. In fact, the painting by artist František Kupka, *Mme Kupka dans les verticales (Mme Kupka among the verticals)* (1910-11), shows literally, as you say, the *disappearing* of the female figure into abstraction. It is the perfect example of the impression or mimeticism of vitality (the female figure), turning *into* the vitality of the author's mark-making. In this case, her husband is painting her out.

Does our Female Genius play with this presence and absence that Graw speaks about? You speak of Mme Kupka as staring out from behind the screen of abstraction:

[I]n this early and officially endorsed abstract painting, the female figure is not separated from and anterior to the abstract marks on the canvas, but is substantially involved in their production. What it means for Madame Kupka, however, is that she is not really there at all.

Is our Female Genius like a genie appearing and disappearing with smoke and screens?

Hey Mel! I'm looking back through our emails to see what the question was. For me, the question started with an absence – as it was in your work – looking for an equivalent character or persona that, no matter how dated it might be (the genius, the master painter) continues to prevail in common currency. So when you start to look for it you find that it's an archetype that just doesn't exist as a specifically female presence in history. It's not so much a question of saying there ARE master female painters and female geniuses, tending in your argument towards building a similar construct to the male version, as much as asking why in the development of these archetypes has there been so much reliance on exclusion? When I started thinking about this I googled female geniuses, because it's such an overblown ridiculous cliché, only to find that the term hardly exists in the positive sense: there was only one book from the '80s and a host of articles saying there's no such thing. Which is when you led me to Battersby's book on gender and genius. It's also partly because in my research on great modern female artists the institution that cropped up the most was

4   Ibid., 80.

the mental institution! So there's a way in which the same things that
   are validated in great men of art or letters (or science to a lesser
   extent) is characterised as mental illness in women, which is largely
   what Battersby writes about. Anyway, the quiz takes a number of these
   biographies (Isa Genzken, Yayoi Kusama, Jean Rhys, Lisa Dwan etc) and
makes a serious joke out of their personal lives and the way their work
   is evaluated to a certain extent along the lines of how well they're
   able to take care of themselves or others, how modest they are, how
   realistic their ideas or fantasies or dreams are etc, etc. It's a list
            of ways of being taken out of the game in a way

Xx Eva

We'll get to the playing field, but first, let's go over the root of this term,
"genius", especially how feminist historian Christine Battersby writes about
it in her book *Gender and Genius* (1990), because I think it touches on the
question of vitality as well.

Here's Battersby on ancient genius, or Roman "geni":

> *For the patrilineal Romans, genius was "a simile for the male seed, which
> from the father begets the son and from the son goes on to continue the
> race". This seed was not simply mundane (physical) sperm; it was a seed
> that was ripened in the bodies of heroic male ancestors, and in the soil that
> had been cleared and planted by generations of males. Genius was a sort of
> genetic coding that entitled a male to property, lands, rights and power over
> women and slaves.*[5]

**Genius is a fluid, what? So embarrassing, right? Didn't
we also start talking about female genius because of
our conversations on your research into the etymology
of the word "embarrassment"?**

Genius comes from "geni" and is linked to a jinn, as in a genie in a bottle, a trickster;
it's also linked to "gene" or genealogy, of course, to the term "genial" and, my favourite:
a bad temper. In my family they say our bad temper has been passed down through our
Sicilian blood, like a feeling of heat and boiling: a flashpoint.

Hey hon no problem. I will edit and make clear this is a developing discussion
between us
This week has been a TOTAL CLUSTERFUCK
Virtual hug
Here's the essay I've been working on that I'm going to read, this sets the stage for
talking about the game of genius, the burning body and liquidity of gestures I think,
xx mel

//

As I wrote in an essay titled *Luxury Goods*, which I sent you, I describe how the con job,
or confidence man, may rob us of material goods, but leave us with a fantasy.

Eva, what does confidence have to do with our Female Genius? Confidence
is the story we believe in, and belief is what we instill our "con"fidence in.
How do we instil value in a mark, which is the embodied form of an artist?
How do we have confidence in this mark, this author? How does our Female
Genius insert herself into the conversation about the vitalist projection of

5   Christine Battersby, *Gender
and Genius: Towards a Feminist
Aesthetics* (Indiana: Indiana
University Press, 1990), 57.

objects and ideas? Who gets to be funny and not serious? Who gets to make fun of themselves because it doesn't imply self-criticism or anxiety?

It makes me think of your question in your essay on my work "Painting Behind Itself": Who gets to be abstract?

Who does get to be abstract? As in who gets to be off-point, random, bad-tempered, who gets to be not-giving-a-fuck, lying, you-don't-have-a-clue anyway, I was just joking, until I'm not, then it's not funny at all, duh?

The inverse of confidence is the con. So, is the inverse of abstraction is literalness, or making sense?

Hey Mel – swamped with work, sorry.
I would say to people who think the term genius is dated that actually the great male painter and the genius are absolutely in common currency and on the rise, by the way! It's very much tied into a neoliberal economic climate that encourages the dismantling of the social network or social welfare state – in a way it's the zenith of the "meritocracy" ideology, where the best will always rise to the top no matter what, because their innate talent will always come through, whether or not they have free education etc.
In fact, the genius character according to that logic is only hindered by the rules and red tape of social provision. Actually, I'd even go so far as to say that a society that really believes in genius in that sense, ironically enough, is a society that elects Trump, because he doesn't need boring advice or expertise or experience or community, it's enough just to have force of personality and is a great story that ignores all the other input that goes into someone doing great things.
Like the myth of the lone cowboy or something.
I'm keen as well to have the term "female genius" be more of a locus of investigation rather than just a hashtag ... on that point I'd agree with Marina Vishmidt: the point is to deconstruct the ideas, not just to go around labeling people geniuses according to the already existing cliché
Ok hope you get the gist of all that
Xx loads of love and let me know if that helps, Eva
Xx

//

This path you describe Eva, is a way well-trodden in feminist history.
The constant battle with representation and value, which is then in turn seen as an embarrassing pursuit.

But what if the vitality of the gesture is inscribed not so much through the character of the artist onto a surface (like a fluid moving through a vessel), but rather the unfolding of events (like the washing of a surface)? What happens to vitality when the story of how authorship projects onto an object isn't told through a conquering-like narrative (splash!), but a wandering discovery (plunk ...)? Does the gene of genealogy rear its head?

//

In art historian and curator Helen Molesworth's 2014 essay, "How to Install Art as a Feminist", she dwells on the conundrum of the genealogies of women and feminist artists:

"Genealogies for art made by women aren't so clear, largely because they are structured by a shadowy absence."[6] One model she suggests is that women artists find the gestures of their often-absent predecessors outside of a timeline, and that they seek "attachment rather than separation", that there is a relational quality between women artists, and that this "releases women to deal with their fathers and encounter their siblings on equal terms".[7]

But what this argument doesn't address is that women's gestures are less valuable than their male peers because their gestures have been accumulated into larger narratives of art history, whilst leaving their authorship out.

Can our Female Genius confront how women artists' productive bodies have been used in a bourgeois system to squeeze their gestures through a sieve, producing the nectar of enlightened "genius" for others?

//

In French, the word "embarrass" meant first of all a blockade or obstruction ... In 1726, the play L'Embarrass des Richesses by the Abbe d'Allainval made known the phrase in French whereby an "embarrassment of" something meant superabundance or excess, of choice, of riches, etc. This use entered English and is still commonly used. For example, "Suddenly, however, we were facing an embarrass de richesses."[8]

Simon Schama, in his book The Embarrassment of Riches: An Interpretation of Dutch Culture in the Golden Age,[9] uses the phrase as a way of understanding a certain discomfort in the Dutch temperament with unprecedented material superabundance, resulting from colonial exploration.[10]

)))))

To embarrass the gesture.
To block or obstruct the movement of something on the move.

But what is this FORCE, right?
When pressure, stress, weight and velocity come into play.
Metabolism of images and material: Squeezed ::: out

//

6 Helen Molesworth, "How to Install Art as a Feminst', in *Women Artists at the Museum of Modern Art*, ed. Cornelia Butler and Alexandra Schwartz (New York, Museum of Modern Art, 2010, 504.
7 Ibid., 505.
8 Margaret Thatcher, *The Downing Street Years* (New York: HarperCollins, 1993).
9 Simon Schama, *The Embarrassment of Riches: An Interpretation of Dutch Culture in the Golden Age* (New York: Alfred A. Knopf, 1987).
10 Eva Kenny, "The 32 Things You Need To Know About Embarrassment – It's an Aesthetic, Not an Emotion", in *PERSONA*, Issue 2, eds. Melissa Gordon and Marina Vishmidt (Berlin: Archive Books, 2013), 56.

I'm interested in the uncontrollability and immeasurability of fluids.

Our Female Genius is also fluid, but not in an "It's cool, things are casual, my schedule is moveable" kind of way. She is fluid in the way she fills the cracks, she's been there, she is there, *she will be there*.

The Gesture is a Liquid

(Originally published in a limited-edition artist book made with designer Daniel Rother in 2017-18. The text and book were completed and presented on the occasion of the exhibition of June 2018, *The Mechanics of Fluids*, for which Gordon curated and developed the scenography in New York.)

A gesture is a liquid. It is liquid, adjective and noun.

Lately I've been thinking that a painting happens
all over the fucking place.
And what if a canvas is just in the way?

Americans call it the support
But nothing is goddamn solid anymore.

Let's take the pulse:
Our brains / block the sound
Of our hearts /
From our ears /
So we don't /
Feel the gush /
of our own materiality.

Some notes on liquids:
Liquids are abstract un-forms, rushing to fill space, existing not specifically here or there, but homogeneously across any expanse. They spread out, slide down, drip, seep, feel WET.
    They push uncontrollably outwards, are messy and immeasurable; liquids are material that *behaves*. They can be measured through their speed, conductibility, and viscosity as much as by volume. Their meaning is to *move*.
    What is this *flow*?

"It is already getting around – at what rate? In what contexts? In spite of what resistances?"[1]

Feminist philosopher Luce Irigaray in her chapter "The 'Mechanics' of Fluids" in the book *The Sex Which is Not One* (1977) outlines the idea of the female *as* a liquid, in that:

"Women diffuse themselves according to modalities scarcely compatible with the framework of the ruling symbolics".[2]

Sorry, what?

OF THE RULING SYMBOLIC$.

Irigaray speaks of the "precedence" given to solids, and also of the potential of liquids to "jam" the works of the theoretical machine, an infection or *affectation* of the surface against which it finds itself walled up.

1 Luce Irigaray, *This Sex Which is Not One* (Ithaca: Cornell University Press, 1985), 106.
2 Ibid.

I am talking about FORM here.

(I mean what, like specifically?) (T W ITC H)

THAT

> it allows itself to be easily traversed by flow by virtue of its conductivity to currents coming from other fluids or exerting pressure through the walls of a solid; THAT it mixes with bodies of a like state, sometimes dilutes itself in them in an almost homogeneous manner, which makes the distinction between the one and the other problematical; and furthermore that it is already diffuse "in itself," which disconcerts any attempt at static identification.[3]

The formlessness of liquids and gestures can be seen in their simultaneous plurality of forms and material ...

(DEEP BREATH)

This gooey, sticky shit stuck between the gaps is formless
(and plural itself):
Formless and excessive.

Throughout my entire life I've been told that

> "Pleasure" – is – to quote Irigaray one last time – the "black-out of meaning".[4]

As in my pleasure, invalidated, because it remains in the realm
of pleasure and never goes to the realm of experience.
    Paint is also a liquid, obviously, but it's often thought of as
a surface that is applied and fixed onto a *picture*.
    How to maintain the liquid-ness of a liquid in a painting?
Is this an act of maintenance?

Mierle Laderman Ukeles, artist-in-residence of the New York City Fresh Kills Landfill since the 1970s, writes in her *Manifesto for Maintenance Art, 1969!*:

> Maintenance is a drag; it takes all the fucking time (LITERALLY!) The mind boggles and CHAFES at the boredom. The culture confers lousy status on maintenance jobs = minimum wages, housewives = no pay. Clean your desk, wash the dishes, clean the floor, wash your clothes, wash your toes, change the baby's diaper, finish the report, correct the typos, mend the fence, keep the customer happy, throw out the stinking garbage, watch out don't put things in your nose, what shall I wear, I have no sox, pay your bills, don't litter, save string, wash your hair, change the sheets, go to the store, I'm out of perfume, say it again – he doesn't understand, seal it again – it leaks, go to work, this art is dusty, clear the table, call him again, flush the toilet, stay young.[5]

EVERYTHING a liquid touches is a CONTAINER.

3 Ibid., 111.
4 Ibid., 114.
5 Mierle Laderman Ukeles, "Manifesto for Maintenance Art 1969! Proposal for an exhibition 'CARE'", *Journal of Contemporary Painting*, 4:2 ([1969] 2018): 233-237.

Its shape-form is defined by what it touches, pushes up against, presses.
Liquids are hot or cold, sticky or slick, and they are pushed around by
objects, walls, pipes: repressed by the architecture containing them.
Shored up. Harnessed,

But ready to burst through at any time.

In this way, surfaces are also containers.

Cropping and containing the ongoing-ness of ongoing movement.

I'm going to diverge, and follow a new conduit. Imagine you are on a boat with me: we're taking a right turn from the main river, but the water behind us, and in all directions, is, as it is in all the world, both a single and plural homogenous mass —existing both in the past and the future, both here and there at the same time.

SIGH. SIP.

My body is a furnace for oxygen and organic material. I am also an ocean, in that systems of liquids are forced around the container of my limbs and skin. It is barely held together. I am pushing out of myself at all moments. Gravity plays a part in my function.

In *"Formless: A User's Guide"* (1997), philosopher Yve-Alain Bois states:

> *Even if one no longer speaks of painting as a "window opened onto the world", the modernist picture is still conceived as a vertical section that presupposes the viewer's having forgotten that his or her feet are in the dirt. Art, according to this view, is a subliminatory activity that separates the perceiver from his or her body.*[6]

What if you're stuck in the mud, eh?

My interest in enacting liquidity is to upset the hierarchy of gestures that might be considered "above all that" daily shit.

> *Just having a body is a daily comedy. From the control tower of the head, one gazes downward, always downward, upon this "loose baggy monster" that we find ourselves in, this laughable casement that is the body below, as ankles swell, farts are emitted, rolls of fat jut out, the penis does its own thing. Shit happens and then you die.*[7]

Artist Amy Sillman often speaks about her paintings as being filmic, having within them a series of film stills, decisions and moves. This embodies for me the most exciting aspect of liquidity: that the liquid movement between states is where a gesture lies in painting.

In philosopher Giorgio Agamben's essay "Notes on Gesture" he tells us that "Cinema leads images back to the homeland of gesture".[8] Agamben asks: what is a gesture? It is something that is "inscribed" into the sphere of action, but is neither acting nor making; it is neither production nor performance. Not the mark and not the act that makes the mark.

> *The gesture is the exhibition of a mediality: it is the process of making a means visible as such. It allows the emergence of the being-in-a-medium of human beings.*[9]

In reading Agamben, I began to understand gesture as the flickering of firelight animating a cave painting of jumping animals, or the frames of a film juddering together to make movement. I am understanding gesture as the imaginative jump in our heads that *believes* in the action that created the physical trace of the event.

6 Yve-Alain Bois and Rosalind E. Krauss, *Formless: A User's Guide* (New York: Zone Books, 1997), 25.

7 Amy Sillman, "Shit Happens", in *Amy Sillman: Faux Pas: Selected Writings and Drawings*, eds. Charlotte Houette, François Lancien-Guilberteau and Benjamin Thorel (Paris: After 8 Books, 2020), 149-150.

8 Giorgio Agamben, "Notes On Gesture", in *Means Without End*, 48-59 (Minneapolis: University of Minnesota Press, 2000), 56.

9 Ibid., 58.

FOUNTAIN

S.Duchamp: apartment,
with readymade suspended
c.1917

It is as if a silent invocation calling for the liberation of the image into gesture arose from the entire history of art. This is what in ancient Greece was expressed by the legends in which statues break the ties holding them and begin to move.[10]

//

I have begun to think of intention as a force that acts on a liquid. An editor once made a comment when I described some paint as "sitting still". "How could it be anything else?", they asked. Like seeing the aftereffects of a flood, I can only see how liquid was moved through space:

"A mark in paint registers the passage of force through matter. Such trajectories evade mimetic representation."[11]

In Mina Loy's poetry; in Lynda Benglis' sculptures; in Josephine Pryde and Eileen Quinlan's photographs; in Sidsel Meineche Hansen's VR videos, sex, fluids and movement take precedence. An ejaculatory joy of fluidity, critical in its excess.

This question of abundance and excess is present in the unseen movement of things in the contemporary world: objects, people, images, money. In artist Hito Steyerl's 2012 e-flux essay "Spam of the Earth: Withdrawal from Representation", she speaks about the insidious relationship between abstract forms of representation that take shape in real and unreal identities.

Visual representation matters, indeed, but not exactly in unison with other forms of representation. There is a serious imbalance between both. On the one hand, there is a huge number of images without referents; on the other, many people without representation. To phrase it more dramatically: A growing number of unmoored and floating images corresponds to a growing number of disenfranchised, invisible, or even disappeared and missing people.[12]

Is this real and abstract un-moored quality of images and personages addressed by recent discussions of representation, in which authorship deals with the liquid boundaries of the self? In terms of belonging, could the liquid-like term "queer" be a way to allow in all those that do not belong to our worlds and subjectivities?

[Writer] Eve Kosofsky Sedgwick wanted to make way for queer to hold all kinds of resistances and fracturings and mismatches that have little or nothing to do with the sexual orientation. "Queer is a continuing moment, movement, motive – recurrent, eddying, troublant," she wrote. "Keenly it is relational, and strange." She wanted the term to be a perpetual excitement, a kind of place-holder – a nominative, like Argo, willing to designate molten or shifting parts, a means of asserting while also giving the slip.[13]

In my thinking, I am linking the ever-renewing and repeating *Argo* ship to the construction of a painting, and its ever-changing life at sea (in an exhibition, a storeroom, an archive, a trash heap). Both embody qualities of re-assemblage, which has been so prevalent in postmodernism, but also in the repetitive re-utterance of a "perpetual excitement". For how else do you keep on painting if not for that itch that tells you something just isn't quite fixed?

10 Ibid., 61.
11 David Joselit, "Resembling Painting", in *Painting 2.0: Expression in the Information Age*, eds. Achim Hochdoerfer, David Joselit and Manuela Ammer (New York: Prestel, 2016), 169.
12 Hito Steyerl, "The Spam of the Earth: Withdrawal from Representation", *e-flux Journal #32* (February 2012): https://www.e-flux.com/journal/32/68260/the-spam-of-the-earth-withdrawal-from-representation/.
13 Maggie Nelson, *The Argonauts* (Minneapolis: Greywolf Press, 2015), 41.

How then, can a gesture ever be simply material?
Or a material good?

//

In November 2011, the night before a Sotheby's auction, Cady Noland disavowed ownership of her work *Cowboys Milking* (1990) (put on auction just after her record auction sale months before), thus effectively erasing millions of dollars from the world. There is no trace of the erasure, though, because those dollars were completely imaginary. Those, say, six million dollars never existed, and they never will exist. It is perhaps one of the best cons in art history.

//

All these funny bodily movements of capital: Burn Rate
Hot Money
Fat Chance, Capital Flows
Absorption Rate, Animal Spirits
Back End.

All moving towards accrual or depletion.
Quantity, no other awareness.

The Embarrassment of SUCKCESS

(Originally delivered as a talk at Witte de With, Rotterdam – since renamed Kunst-instituut Melly – on 24 April 2019 on the occasion of the exhibition *An exhibition with an audio script by Sarah Demuse and Wendy Tronrud, as well as a soundtrack by Mario Garcia Torres in collaboration with Sol Oosel*. The talk was turned into a published artwork with then Witte de With director Sofía Hernández Chong Cuy, as a limited-edition four-part mail-out poster, with Kunstinstituut Melly in 2020.)

In the run-up to her eviction from her Grand Street loft (possibly in 1972), artist Lee Lozano began writing a large number of "pieces" in her small private notebooks: *No Parties Piece, No Eating Out Piece*, and more famously her *General Strike Piece* and *Boycott Women Piece*. There is no formal translation from diary to the written A4 instructional *Dropout Piece* (begun circa 1970), like many other Lozano dematerialised art works of the late 1960s and early 1970s. Rather, at the tail end of her notebooks (in which she worked from 1967 to 1970), Lozano acknowledges that the "action" is already underway when she writes, *"Dropout Piece is the hardest work I have ever done."*

In "Lee Lozano, 68, Conceptual Artist Who Boycotted Women for Years", art critic Roberta Smith's 1999 obituary for Lozano in *The New York Times*, she describes the edge on which Lozano walked in the execution of her work:

> *"In the mid-1960s she also began to execute a series of life-related actions (she didn't like the word performance) that tested, among other things, her stamina, her friends' patience and the conduct of everyday life."*

//

An instruction is a basic component of conceptual practices, and one that usually involves a command to an "other": a friend, a machine, a worker, an intern. The body in much conceptual work is present (for example in Chris Burden's artwork *Shoot* of 1971) as the one person who would *dare* to do it. Lozano, though, inverted this: she instructed herself in actions, and dared everyone else to *put up with it.* In Sarah Lehrer Graiwer's meticulously researched book *Dropout Piece* (2014), she notes this entry in Lozano's notebook just before her eviction:

> *"LYING ON BED SMOKING, EMPTYING MIND, LISTENING TO RACHMANINOV IN DIM (CITYPOOR) LIGHTBULB A FEELING OF PEACE COMES OVER ME, OF JOYOUS FREEDOM, OF IM DOING WHAT I WANT, OF I DON'T HAVE TO DO ANYTHING UNTIL I FEEL LIKE IT (...) DROP OUT FROM WORLD, NO CALLS NO WORK NO OBLIGATIONS NO GUILT NO DESIRES, JUST MY MIND WANDERING LAZILY OFF ITS LEASH. THIS EVIDENTLY IS THE ONLY WAY TO TAKE A REST."*[1]

Let's take a deep breath.
(Bend over, breathe slowly coming up,
arms hanging down, let the gravity work.)
Breathe.
Breathe.

1   Lehrer-Graiwer, Lee Lozano: Dropout Piece, 74.

Lozano's note feels especially pertinent in this contemporary moment: How can I rest in and amongst what is now called "work" as an artist?

And how can I do so when I'm expected to be switched *on* all the time, even in relaxation mode?

With the expectation that an artist shouldn't work TOO hard.

//

In my essay "Presence and Absence" I wrote:

Increasingly as an artist I have begun to feel my voice becoming disembodied from myself. Who is it that is "speaking"? It is strange to envision oneself as a construct, a concept, outside of one's own body, but that is exactly what is perceived by others: an accumulation of objects, made by a non-entity with a vague persona, skewed and squared by gestures and contexts.

In the essay, I speak about four female artists: Cady Noland, Lee Lozano, Charlotte Posenenske and Laurie Parsons. I describe them as literally walking off the edge of the art world, revealing the edges of the playing field to which they were confined at the time.

I am not interested in Lee Lozano, Charlotte Posenenske or Laurie Parsons for their obscurity. I do not believe the myths that they were "not able to hack it". Perhaps they were smart enough to wash their hands of the situation they found themselves in, but regardless, each of their gestures expanded the role of authorship because their actions existed outside of the playing field of art. The act of dropping out was simply the natural conclusion to their work: they took their practice to the extreme of authorship, then followed through.

//

Dropping out is a gesture of walking out. A strike. A Human Strike.[2]

Dropouts walk out off the edge of the world in which they exist at the time: off the map, off the grid. As a character for others to see, the dropout acts outside the bounds of the playing field of contemporary art, and by doing so, reveals the shape-form of the container: when the boundaries that hold these gestures become immaterial.

What is this shape-form, this container, of gestures?

//

It takes a shift in perception to consider dropping out as an act or a gesture instead of a circumstance. To do this requires the removal of an artist's biography from the understanding of their work. This is often hard when many women artists, especially those who have "exited" the art world they were living in to go into exile, are shrouded in mystique (Agnes Martin, Sonia Delaunay, Jo Baer, Joan Mitchell).

Let's be clear: dropping out was unfashionable for all these women. Terms like "failure", "disturbed", "forgotten", "sad", "drug-addict" were used.

Post-partum, I feel it in my stomach, the dark hole that has always been there. It makes me so sad I can't tell you.

2   Claire Fontaine, *The Human Strike Has Already Begun & Other Essays* (London: Mute, 2013).

48

Let's not ignore the moment in time in which we live in relationship to this:

Forgotten or undervalued women artists can encourage a sense of "discovery", a cat and mouse play: the finding of hidden histories as gems that we, in the art world are trying to uncover like truffle pigs. If we, though, consider, that historically the condition of dropout was common and expected for women artists, the conundrum of presence and absence becomes more fraught, especially in a reevaluation or revaluation of these female "rarities."

Why this sudden valuation of that which must be FOUND?

Women artists! Come out from under there! Stop hiding under your chairs! Curators and gallerists, they can't find you down there!

//

The cover of the October 8, 2018, issue of *The New Yorker* shows a silencing red hand over the mouth of a female face, exactly one year after the Harvey Weinstein scandal "broke". Inside, in the heart-wrenching article, "The Canvas Ceiling", a review by the writer Claudia Roth Pierpont of the book *Ninth Street Women* (2018), there is a description of the group of women painters – Grace Hartigan, Helen Frankenthaler, Joan Mitchell, Elaine de Kooning and Lee Krasner – who were present in and partners of the New York School group of painters, together at the opening of an exhibition of painter Willem De Kooning's *Women* paintings:

> *"In 1953 – in a fancy midtown gallery that did not show women painters – [they] blithely offered their own observations: 'That one's you. That one's me.'"*[3]

//

In the process of writing about gesture recently, I've been imagining gestures as liquids, especially gestures that evade a neat stacking like so many Amazon boxes in underpaid un-unionised warehouses. Gestures as liquids moving between things. I began to imagine what happens when these gestures become TOO MUCH; when they start pushing out, forcing things around.

//

Originally, the term "embarrassment" implied an excess or overabundance. And the shame that evolved to contain the fear of such leaking.

To "embarrass" the gesture.

To block or obstruct the movement of something on the move.

But what is this *force*?

When pressure, stress, weight and velocity come into play.

Slap the floor with something rubbery, slap my legs?

> *A mark / in paint / registers / the passage /of force / through mat/ter."*[4]
> *[My breaks.]*

3   Claudia Roth Pierpont, "The Canvas Ceiling", *The New Yorker* (8 October 2018), 478.
4   Joselit, "Reassembling Painting", 169.

//

Let's go back to the moment I saw Mary Heilmann's paintings for the first time.

They shot me down like a bolt to the head, which was followed closely by an acute sense of sadness. (At making it to almost 30 years old as a painter through multiple art schools without encountering her work).

That night, one of the last that I lived in Berlin in 2008, I sat down and wrote:

Perseverance makes me sad.

In a June 2016 article in *The Guardian*, Jason Farago wrote about Heilmann:

> *In case it's not evident, Heilmann knows a lot of people in the art world. But after years of underexposure for her own work, the US artist is finally enjoying a welcome career surge in her eighth decade ... This attention is belated validation of Heilmann's talents. Spend time in her light-filled studio in New York, however, and you'll soon discover she was never out of the picture.*[5]

Heilmann has been around, yes, but that doesn't mean she hasn't been subjected to the "endless low-level harassment" as a woman painter once described it to me, as shown in this interview with painter Ross Bleckner:

> *RB: Yeah. You were showing at Holly Solomon Gallery. And what was funny about your paintings is that they were simple – squares within squares, kind of quasi-minimalist, brightly colored – everything was slightly off register, even the shape of the canvas itself, right? The square would be lopsided.*
> *MH: I don't think so, not on purpose anyway. The interior square –*
> *RB: Well maybe the interior square set up a perception that made me think of it as being slightly ... goofy.*[6]

//

Early one morning, I left a friend's house to go to work, to teach. Walking past artist Phyllida Barlow's house to the Finsbury Park tube station, London, under the bridge past the metal fences that stood where the recently evicted, mainly female homeless community had been, I saw a large poster of dancer Pina Bausch with the words "SHE PERSISTED." No, I thought, NO. I refuse persistence. I refuse the valorisation of waiting your turn.

We should appreciate older women artists for their brilliant practices and lives, we should acknowledge those who have been left out. I shall not celebrate their acceptance as an end unto itself. Instead, I demand that a change must happen to the container itself; their gestures must burst the walls, and as the philosopher Luce Irigaray implies, go everywhere.

//

The notion of woman as a "leaky vessel" is addressed in the final essay in Anne Carson's book of poetry *Glass Irony and God*. Focusing on the role of women's voices in the *polis* in Ancient Greek writing, it is full of examples of the fear and – interestingly – the *loneliness* that female voices produce for men. She describes these sounds:

5   Jason Farago, "Interview: Artist Mary Heilmann: the Californian surfer still making waves in her 70s", *The Guardian* (6 June 2016), https://www.theguardian.com/artanddesign/2016/jun/06/maryheilmann-unsung-heroine-american-art-david-hockney.

6   Ross Bleckner and Mary Heilmann, "Mary Heilmann by Ross Bleckner", *BOMB Magazine* (April 1, 1999), https://bombmagazine.org/articles/mary-heilmann/.

Madness and witchery as well as bestiality are conditions commonly associated with the use of the female voice in public ... there is the heart chilling groan of the Gorgon ... a guttural animal howl that issues a great wind from the back of the throat through a hugely distended mouth.[7]

(Note the quantities in that description.)

The Furies ... high-pitched and horrendous voices ... the deadly voice of the Sirens and the dangerous ventriloquism of Helene ... the incredible babbling of Kassandra ... and the fearsome hullabaloo of Artemis as she charges through the woods ... the seductive discourse of Aphrodite which is so concrete an aspect of her power that she can wear it on her belt as a physical object or lend it to other women ... Iambe who shrieks obscenities and throws her skirt up over her head to expose her genitalia ... the nymph Echo... described by Sophocles as "the girl with no door on her mouth".[8]

Carson writes of the upper and lower mouth ascribed to women. At one point she describes how psychologist Joseph Breuer withheld a publication on his case studies of hysteria and "the talking cure", when he found one of his case studies, Anna O, contorted in the pains of childbirth (with his child), upon opening the door to commence their last meeting.

Carson then writes:

"It is confusing and embarrassing to have two mouths. Genuine kakophony *is the sound produced by them."*[9]

It is *this* history of voice that I keep in mind when I think about the question "who is speaking?" in relation to painting and gesture. Especially, the sense of "two mouths" in relation to the projection of the author onto a painting.

//

Speech is spoken about in the contemporary discourse of painting by writer and editor Isabelle Graw, as something that is projected through the "liveliness" of painting, or vice-versa, that the voice projected through painting brings it to life.

Speech, in this instance, is associated with the body of the painting, a replacement for an absent author whose body is not an *issue.* A body who speaks clearly in the polis.

//

Feminist art historians discuss how women artists' genealogies are haunted by absences. Is it a condition and a strategy to disappear behind the canvas.

//

Dear Eva
Your title, "Painting BEHIND Itself", is about an absent author who remains physically present, though hidden. As I remember, it began when you told me about a piece of writing you had started about what is considered the first abstract painting in history. This painting, *Mme Kupka Amongst Verticals*[10] consists of marks painted on top of, and obscuring, a female figure. In fact, the painting, you say, literalises the disappearing of the female figure into abstraction. It is the perfect example of

7 Anne Carson, Glass,
Irony and God (New York:
New Directions Paperbook,
1995), 120. 7
8 Ibid., 121.
9 Ibid., 135.
10 *Mme Kupka Among Verticals*
(1910-11, oil on canvas) is a
painting by František Kupka
held in the MoMA collection,
New York. It is said to be the
first completely non-figurative
painting, https://www.moma.
org/collection/works/79971.

the impression of vitality (the female figure), turning into the vitality of the author's mark-making. To quote you, "in this early and officially endorsed abstract painting, the female figure is not separated from and anterior to the abstract marks on the canvas, but is substantially involved in their production. What it means for Madame Kupka, however, is that she is not really there at all."[11]

//

In much discourse on contemporary female painters' terms such as "unknowability" (Helen Molesworth) and "unquantifiability" (curator Mark Godfrey) prevail:

> *This lineage raises the question of whether we can locate a feminist position in this approach to abstraction. Molesworth, for one, has already pushed for the term unknowability in a 2013 essay on [Amy] Sillman: "For me, feminism is a critique of power and mastery, and most of all it's a warning about how the combination of mastery and power has, historically, led to violence. One result of this questioning of power is that unknowability emerges as a kind of virtue."[12]*

//

Who gets to be abstract?

Who does get to be abstract? As in who gets to be off-point, random, bad-tempered, who gets to be not-giving-a-fuck, lying, you-don't-have-a-clue anyway, I was just joking, until I'm not, then it's not funny at all: duh?

//

I am a female painter. I have two mouths, I guess, and so I must speak twice about the same things and my speech is confusing.

//

There is an assumption that if you are not successful you are stupid or unlucky.

That if you are poor then you are lazy or ill-suited.

Judgement is built into our systems of appraisal and approval.

In personality tests you are asked: do you empathise with others? Do you see yourself as better than others?

What makes things good in the art world? Being better, speaking better? Since when did this capitalistic tendency infect this community? Is it to do with the pressure to suckceed?

//

> *The team at Studio Olafur Eliasson consists of about ninety people, from craftsmen and specialised technicians, to architects, archivists*

11 Kenny, "Painting Behind Itself", 11.
12 Mark Godfrey, "Statement of Intent", *Artforum* (April 2014): 299.

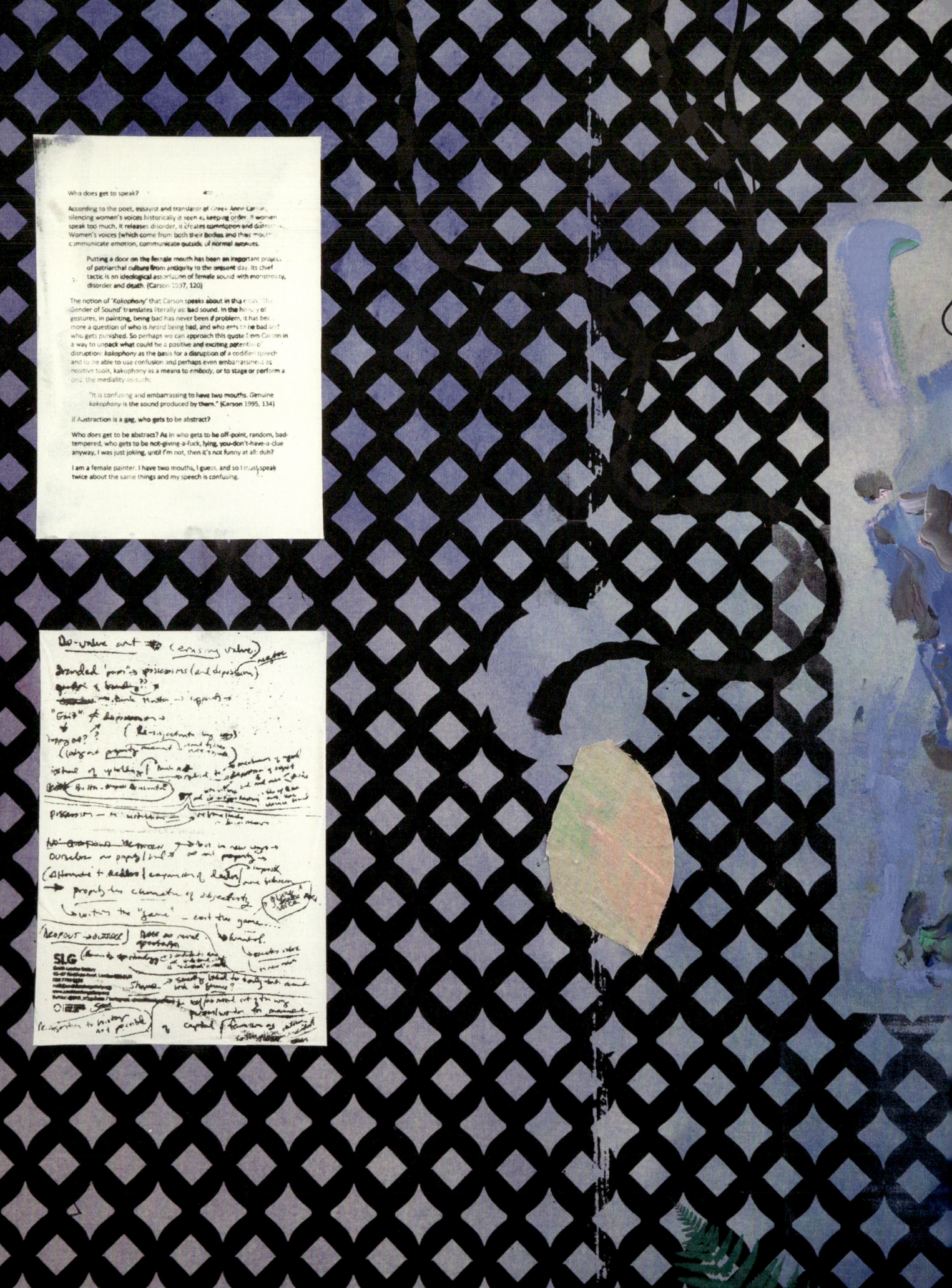

Who does get to speak?

According to the poet, essayist and translator of Greek Anne Carson, silencing women's voices historically is seen as keeping order. If women speak too much, it releases disorder, it creates commotion and distraction. Women's voices (which come from both their bodies and their mouths) communicate emotion, communicate outside of normal avenues.

> Putting a door on the female mouth has been an important project of patriarchal culture from antiquity to the present day. Its chief tactic is an ideological association of female sound with monstrosity, disorder and death. (Carson 1997, 120)

The notion of 'Kakophony' that Carson speaks about in this essay 'The Gender of Sound' translates literally as: bad sound. In the history of gestures, in painting, being bad has never been a problem, it has been more a question of who is heard being bad, and who gets to be bad and who gets punished. So perhaps we can approach this quote from Carson in a way to unpack what could be a positive and exciting potential of disruption: kakophony as the basis for a disruption of a codified speech and to be able to use confusion and perhaps even embarrassment as positive tools, kakophony as a means to embody, or to stage or perform a a once the mediality-as-such:

> "It is confusing and embarrassing to have two mouths. Genuine kakophony is the sound produced by them." (Carson 1995, 134)

If Austraction is a gag, who gets to be abstract?

Who does get to be abstract? As in who gets to be off-point, random, bad-tempered, who gets to be not-giving-a-fuck, lying, you-don't-have-a-clue anyway, I was just joking, until I'm not, then it's not funny at all: duh?

I am a female painter. I have two mouths, I guess, and so I must speak twice about the same things and my speech is confusing.

and art historians, web and graphic designers, filmmakers, cooks, and administrators. They work with Eliasson to develop, produce, and install artworks, projects, and exhibitions, as well as on experimentation, archiving, research, publishing, and communications. In addition to realising artworks in-house, Eliasson and the studio work with structural engineers and other specialists and collaborate worldwide with cultural practitioners, policymakers, and scientists. The studio hosts workshops and events in order to further artistic and intellectual exchanges with people and institutions outside the art world.[13]

At the start of 2015, Koons's studio employed more than 100 painters, some of which were tasked with working on his "Gazing Ball" series, which features blue orbs alongside reproductions of Old Masters paintings. But, according to a 2017 Artnet News report, "lackluster" sales for works from the series, which has been shown at David Zwirner and Gagosian galleries in New York, forced the studio to scale back its operations. In late 2015, around 30 employees were laid off. The following year, the blog Art F City reported that Koons's studio had let go of 15 employees amid attempts by its workers to form a union.[14]

//

A fief, in medieval times, was an item – usually property with unpaid workers attached to it – granted in exchange for a fee, usually consisting of allegiance, homage or service.

//

In 2017 I went to see the exhibition of small paintings of cocks and cunts from the early 1960s by Lee Lozano at Hauser & Wirth, London.[15] I was struck by the strong sense that these works had been in storage, somewhere, for a long time. They were arranged, strangely, from small to large (being very small to about A4 sized). Lozano, fully aware of scale (as in her *Waves* (1967-70) series), may have made these privately, and then someone must have held on to them for decades after her work was moved around (and much of it lost) in the early 1970s. They were installed as embarrassing pictures. They painted Lozano as someone furtive, mad, a take on an artist who in fact was astutely aware of the psychology of contemporary artistic dialogue and endeavoured to make large ground-breaking paintings. These small, early works of Lozano were installed next to a show of artist Ida Applebroog paintings, as if to underscore the point about mental health. When I approached the young woman at the desk to ask about the Lee Lozano *Notebook* for sale – an exact to-scale facsimile with the handwritten words "PRIVATE BOOK #1" on the cover, she excitedly told me that all the notebooks are being made into facsimiles, for sale to the public, and that should I have any interest, all of the notebooks are scanned and available for research in the offices of Hauser and Wirth Gallery, anytime!

//

I'm a failure. No, I am. You might laugh or not think so, it's ok. I've just actually realised this.

Someone I loved dearly passed away recently. They were a complete dropout. They had no job, they had no money, no

13 Olafur Eliasson, "About Studio Olafur Eliasson," https://olafureliasson. net/studio. https://olafureliasson.net/studio, last accessed 10 November 2019.

14 Alex Greenberger, "Jeff Koons Studio Moves to Hudson Yards Amid Layoffs", *Artnews*, 15 January 2019, https://www.artnews.com/art-news/news/moving-offices-hudson-yards-jeff-koons-studiolays-off-employees-11695/.

15 *Lee Lozano, c. 1962*, Hauser & Wirth, London, UK, 19 May – 29 July 2017.

home. They refused to participate in a pressurised
system. They refused not to be alive each day.
Until they weren't anymore.

I've realised that if I don't start living without the
expectations of success, I'm going to be a failure in
so many other ways.

//

> The dropout is a negative character, in the sense of creating negative space
> around an oversight of value. Pulling back a surface, erasing your own
> gestures, holding back information, making holes that move into other
> dimensions, confusing the sense of the real because the real does not
> include you.
>   I took the dropout pill to see freedom of movement. A radical thing:
> something with no value to exchange, no information to cull, just a gesture,
> for all that's worth.

//

Let's not forget that Lozano did not leave New York City after being evicted from her
loft (in 1972 most likely) and starting *Dropout Piece*. According to Lehrer-Graiwer's book
Dropout Piece, she stayed in the city until the free lunches at Max's Kansas City ended ten
years later, in 1983. She hung out at the venue CBGBs (opened in 1973), she affected an
aesthetic along with musicians Patti Smith and the Ramones (I can't help but think of the
commodification of this aesthetic by MTV only a few years later). She danced, she posed,
she drifted along,

   "JUST (HER) MIND WANDERING LAZILY OFF ITS LEASH."[18]

16 Lehrer-Graiwer, *Lee Lozano:
Dropout Piece*, 74.

On Monsters

(Originally delivered as a spoken tour at WIELS Center for Contemporary Art, as part of the "Look Who's Talking" series, on 16 June 2021, in Jacqueline de Jong's painting exhibition *The Ultimate Kiss*.)

I am struck by the act of a woman from the 1960s painting images of female monsters.

I wanted to ask: who are these monsters (the artist, her enemies, all women?), where do they come from (dreams, psychology, or something experienced?) and what does it mean for a painter who started her career in the transition between materially driven versus conceptually driven painting to be haunted by or maybe obsessed with these forms?

I am struck by how monsters are embedded in various gestures in this exhibition: in paintings of accidents, of mass destruction, in references to tragedy, in mess.

This interest in monsters is a longer and larger question for me. Perhaps there is a connection in that I too am a painter, a woman and a printmaker, but I think it is also wrapped up simply in the act of speaking – and I will address here how I equate speaking with painting – and how the role of aesthetic translation of speech is a necessary means by which to speak out of bounds.

//

What is a monster? Before Mary Shelley's emotionally assembled monster in her novel *Frankenstein* (1818), monsters were almost exclusively conceived as an unexpected combination of various animal and human attributes that also entail a voice and bad sounds – something transgressing a boundary.

I have been drawn for years to the description of woman as a "leaky vessel" by writer and translator Anne Carson, paraphrasing the Ancient Greeks. Women were seen as containers: of family secrets, of the fertile ground of a womb that passed on the "gene" of the men's lineage (the right to lands, inherited through the male line). Women were moved to the families of their husbands like vessels, but dangerous with their potential agency: they could be filled with honey, wine or poison.

Speech, which Carson describes as causing fear and even loneliness when used by female subjects in many Greek myths, has more recently been used by the critic Isabelle Graw as a way to understand the liveliness of painting. Her discussion of painterly gesture as imbuing speech and thus life into painting, is a straightforward understanding of the transmission of authorship through the artist's body.

But in the history of gesture that projects speech, not all speech has been seen as good speech, not all speech is seen as logical, or even within the discourse of *the public*. Much female speech has been read as shrill, mad, angry, annoying, prudish, funny, dumb, background noise.

In her essay "Dirt and Desire: Essay on the Phenomenology of Female Pollution in Antiquity",[1] Carson outlines where monstrous women come from, linking the notion of monstrosity to the idea of pollution, or dirt. She does this by pointing out that something is only dirty if it is *in the wrong place*.

Carson begins:

1   Anne Carson, "Dirt and Desire: Essay on the Phenomenology of Female Pollution in Antiquity," in *Men in the Off Hours* (New York: Alfred A. Knopf, 2000).

"Contact is crisis. As the anthropologists say, 'Every touch is a modified blow'... The difficulty presented by any instance of contact is that of violating a fixed boundary, transgressing a closed category where one does not belong." [2]

//

I think of it like this: in my shopping bag might be bleach, cheese, socks, milk, candles, matches, tomatoes and toilet paper. I often imagine the mess that would seep out if the thin plastic or metal containers holding back the interiors of these incompatible items disappeared.

Over time all elements make their way towards becoming dirt. As Carson reminds us, a poached egg on your plate is not dirt, but when it is on the floor of the library, it has transgressed a boundary, and historically, society has instituted rules in order to contain this leaking.

"In such a society, individuals who are regarded as specially lacking in control of their own boundaries, or as possessing special talents and opportunities for confounding the boundaries of others, evoke fear and controlling action from the rest of society." [3]

I began outlining these thoughts in an essay in 2020, where I tried to read the idea of the monstrous voice through the story of myself in 2007, when I felt most out of place. I was a young painter who had left America years previously. I was spending time in libraries researching a show on monstrous depictions of women in feminist publications from the 1970s as a way to deal with having no community myself. That summer, I got married and then went to live alone in an already foreign New York.

What do we do when we feel out of place? What do we have to do in order to feel in the right place, when there isn't a right place for us?

In the essay, I talk about abandoning the "content" of feminism that summer of 2007, because even though it was something I felt deeply connected to, I could see, as an artist, that I was being limited to a fenced-off territory: that I was expected to make work about the topic of feminism because that was *all* I could speak about, that that was the only space in which my voice belonged, and I decided that I would go *out of bounds*.

I enacted this through a series of transitions, which began with a show on monsters, and ended up most recently in work about stolen gestures of modernism. Over the past 15 years, I've made jumps between content and position, sometimes in the same exhibition (blowing up the crumbling surfaces of modernist paintings, silk-screening large-scale installations, photographing and re-painting my own unconscious painting marks, making huge paintings about gesture). Maybe these combinations were confusing, because changes are awkward for others, because others want you to speak with one voice.

//

In the book *Can the Monster Speak?: A Report to an Academy of Psychoanalysts* (2021) the writer Paul B. Preciado speaks at length about gender transitioning. The book is based on a lecture that Preciado tried to deliver, as a trans person, to the Society of Psychologists in Paris, where he was shouted off the stage and publicly humiliated: silenced.

Preciado outlines the problems – and especially the contemporary shift – of sexual difference: "I would like to begin by saying that the regime of sexual difference as promulgated by psychoanalysis is neither a natural nor a symbolic order but an epistemological politics of the body and that, as such, it is historical and changing." [4]

2 Ibid., 130.
3 Ibid., 131.
4 Paul B. Preciado, *Can the Monster Speak?: A Report to an Academy of Psychoanalysts* (London: Fitzcarraldo Editions, 2021), 26.

1. _____ gestures.
Puzzle pieces
Keys and keyholes
Cutout . . . . string . . .
Rubbing on back of canvas.
Strings, like Picasso's guitar. Like Braque or
Pockets
_____
Fruit . . .
Mesh trays.
Hooks
Cutout shapes . . . .
Animal spirits
Create . . . .
. . . .
. . . .

. . . .
Black . . . . edge
Hang . . . . . .
Wheat . . . . to wall
Mesh . . . . . .
Wood . . . .
Same as . . . .
Circle . . . .

Preciado's book opens up a space for monsters; it celebrates the fact of not being one or the other, not being in the right place, because there is NO RIGHT PLACE TO BE:

Mimetism is a poor tool when thinking about gender transition since it still relies on binary logic. To be this or that, to be one thing and imitate something else. (THIS IS THE HISTORY OF THE MONSTER.) Either you are a man, or you are a woman. A trans person is not imitating anything, just as a crocodile is not imitating a floating tree trunk, or a chameleon the colors of the world. To be trans is to cease to be a crocodile and connect with one's own vegetal future, to understand that the rainbow can become a skin.[5]

The monster is also inherently – as Preciado states – a being through time. The monster embodies the right to change and keep changing. Monsters historically are representations of the fears and obsessions of their age, and have been inherently linked to notions of "evil" (perhaps because they represent change, which is feared).

In her essay "Towards a Metalanguage of Evil", artist Cady Noland outlines the idea that "in America there is a meta-game". I have always taken her essay to be a critique of the art world, since it was published in the Documenta IX catalogue and I think when Noland lays out a psychopathic relationship between and an X and a Y in the essay, she is talking about gender, about power, about difference, and the game of difference, the game of authorship (and celebrity).

Noland begins her essay by stating that "The rules of the game, or even that there is a game at all, are hidden to some."[6] She continues by describing in an oblique manner a relationship between X and Y, in which X is constantly, in a Tom and Jerry-like scenario, trying to con Y, citing references to many contemporaneous tropes of media culture in America.

It's important to note that Noland sets out the notion of "evil" as a game or device, so it's key to keep in mind that the essay is not a reading of a situation or a metaphor but exists purely as a theoretical overview of potential moves or gestures. She's not talking about herself or the art world as such, but rather a practice and the playing field in which all gestures can be situated.

I'm not talking abstractly here.

At the opening of Amy Sillman's show *Landline* at Camden Arts Centre,[7] which I attended to write a review for *Texte Zur Kunst*, the audience gathered in small groups, often in the corners of the room, talking and periodically staring at their phones together. It was only later, at the dinner, that I remembered that in Washington D.C., five hours behind us, was the live-streaming of the testimony of Christine Blasey-Ford against Bret Kavanaugh for sexual assault.[8] Sillman was encouraged to give a speech at the opening dinner: she stood up and quickly gave a dedication to Blasey-Ford. When she'd finished, up shot a white-haired British man, who, perhaps drunkenly, shouted, "Innocent until proven guilty!" and quickly sat down again.

Earlier, standing in the galleries, an older, male British painter asked me how I was able to read the work. It was the same artist who had previously told me how Laura Owens' painting "just wasn't serious". He was confused by the variety of approaches, the temporal shifts and references. There was no hook, and no handle for him because of a refusal to inhabit the position of "one", the position of arriving at an endpoint for all to see. I saw him sitting next to the artist's New York gallerist at the dinner, talking in her ear.

5   Ibid., 27.
6   Noland, "Towards a Metalanguage of Evil", 410.
7   Amy Sillman, *Landline*, Camden Arts Centre, London, 28 September – 6 January 2019.
8   On 27 September 2018, the psychology professor Dr Christine Blasey-Ford testified to the Senate Judiciary Committee in the United States that then Supreme Court nominee Bret Kavanaugh had sexually assaulted her 36 years previously.

//

There are monsters everywhere, but only some of us sound bad.

//

So, what happens when we speak badly in painting? What happens when we try to speak badly and it is seen as embarrassing, when we try to speak intelligently, and it is seen as trying too hard? What happens when our subjective point of view is impossible to inhabit? Who wants to be only one thing anyway?

And then, what about women who speak badly because they are not in solidarity with other women, because they believe that aligning themselves with power structures gives them power over other women? (But then want to talk to you about it when it all backfires.)

I recently revisited the comedian Michelle Wolf's stand-up comedy at the White House Correspondents Association dinner in 2019, and her descriptons of the women in the Trump administration:

We should definitely talk about the women in the Trump administration ... There's also, of course, Ivanka. She was supposed to be an advocate for women, but it turns out she's about as helpful to women as an empty box of tampons. She's done nothing to satisfy women, so I guess, like father, like daughter. Oh, you don't think he's good in bed? Come on! [9]

Who were the monsters in Jacqueline de Jong's paintings? They are REAL. To me, aesthetically, her oil paintings from the 1960s resemble De Kooning's *Women* paintings.

As described in Mary Gabriel's book *Ninth Street Women* (2017), when the group of female painters – rightly famous and highly regarded amongst their peers, both supportive and competitive with each other – Grace Hartigan, Helen Frankenthaler, Joan Mitchell, Elaine de Kooning and Lee Krasner – stand together at the opening of an exhibition of De Kooning's *Women* paintings:

"In 1953 – in a fancy midtown gallery that did not show women painters – [they] blithely offered their own observations: 'That one's you. That one's me.'" [10]

Perhaps, this identification with the monster is the most interesting potential – seeing a representation of self as a being who speaks (makes, looks, behaves) out of bounds no matter how hard you try: how could we *not* identify with them? They are depictions of us.

It is the world that must change to hear the monster speaking.

9   Michelle Wolf at the White House Correspondents dinner, 29 April 2018.
10 Mary Gabriel, *Ninth Street Women, Lee Krasner, Elaine de Kooning, Grace Hartigan, Joan Mitchell and Helen Frankenthaler: Five Painters and the Movement That Changed Modern Art* (London: Little Brown and Company, 2017), 478.

Liquid Gestures: The Language of That Land

(Originally delivered as a talk at the symposium *No Rules* at Camberwell School of Art, London, on 26 March 2022. The symposium was organised to explore the exhibition *Helen Frankenthaler: Radical Beauty*, a survey of the American artist's woodcuts at the Dulwich Picture Gallery, London.)

We can locate at the basis of many "seminal" painterly moments a literal primitive accumulation, a "reaping" of the value of another's gestures, and often the appropriation of elements of a female artist's practice by their male peers. It appears that critic Clement Greenberg was in fact the conductor of two such moments in high modernist painting history. It is worth beginning this essay with both instances, presented as short anecdotes, as an introduction to how we might begin to address aesthetic language in relationship to a painter such as Helen Frankenthaler, on which so little official painting terminology has been focused.

Here's the first smoking gun, which describes how Greenberg and his protégé artist Jackson Pollock saw the "drips" of the artist Janet Sobel a year before Pollock began his "breakthrough" gestures in late summer 1946: on page 218 of "American Type Painting" in *Partisan Review*, 1955, Clement Greenberg writes:

> *Back in 1944, however, he [Pollock] had noticed one or two curious paintings shown at Peggy Guggenheim's [Art of this Century Gallery] by a "primitive" painter, Janet Sobel (who was and still is, a housewife living in Brooklyn). Pollock (and I myself) admired these pictures rather furtively: they showed schematic little drawings of faces almost lost in a dense tracery of thin black lines lying over and under a mottled field of predominantly warm and translucent color. The effect – and it was the first really "all-over" one that I had ever seen ... was strangely pleasing. Later on, Pollock admitted that these pictures had made an impression on him.*[1]

In another account, the same Greenberg took painters Morris Louis and Kenneth Noland into Frankenthaler's studio on West 23rd Street in New York in April 1953 to show them her new "soak stain" painting technique, in which Frankenthaler used the spread of thinned paint on raw canvas:

> *The night of April 4, Clem invited a group of people to his Bank Street apartment for drinks. Several artists [...] among them a former student of Clem's at Black Mountain, Kenneth Noland, and his painter friend Morris Louis. He asked the group if they would like to see something new. He noted in his appointment book that day: "At 6pm Louis & Noland, along with Chas, Egan, George McNeil, Franz Kline, Leon and Ida Berkowitz & Margaret Brown and I visited Helen Frankenthaler's studio, where some of us stayed until 11." Helen wasn't there. Clem chose that moment to introduce his guests to her painting* Mountains and Sea.[2]

Greenberg then encouraged both Louis and Noland's practices, where they each developed "poured" colour-field techniques, writing about and promoting them, leaving Frankenthaler largely out of the narrative until the exhibition *Post Painterly Abstraction* held at the Los Angeles County Museum of Art in 1964.

What can a 2023 reader make of these anecdotes, with all our hindsight of the funding of exhibitions of abstraction by the American national security

1   Clement Greenberg [1955], "American-Type Painting", in *Art and Culture: Critical Essays* (Boston: Beacon Press, 1961), 218.
2   Gabriel, *Ninth Street Women*, 478.

apparatus,[3] the corporate legacy of the collecting of modern art, and the contemporary re-hanging of large art collections such as MoMA and Tate Britain to reflect practices coming from outside the centre of this high modern canon? Why does looking at the theft or "borrowing" of female artists' gestures as central to the main development of painting history matter now?

We can add these two revised "creation" stories of the drip and colour field to the ongoing debate and discussion around the authorship of the 1917 *Fountain* submitted to the Society of Independent Artists. As is discussed on the Tate website, Baroness Elsa von Freitag-Loringhoven, a German-born contemporary of Marcel Duchamp, may perhaps have submitted the urinal as a political protest against the entering of America into WWI.[4] I conclude from these stories that the "reaped" gestures (the Baroness' readymade, Sobel's drips, Frankenthaler's soak-stain colour fields) were considered in and of themselves *so important*, and distinct from their authors, that a narrative had to be created in order to present them (the gestures) with some form of "reputational" push.

My first encounter with one of Frankenthaler's woodcuts, which were the focus of the exhibition *Helen Frankenthaler: Radical Beauty* at Dulwich Picture Gallery in London in 2021, was whilst I was organising a group exhibition entitled *The Mechanics of Fluids* at Marianne Boesky Gallery in New York in 2018. In *The Mechanics of Fluids,* I was attempting to unfold an alternative history of how to view abstract gesture in painting through a more liquid, moveable understanding of the motivations of abstraction. I had secured works by almost all the historic and contemporary artists I had chosen. These were assembled to place women artists' practices at the forefront of the notion of liquidity in the history of abstraction, so it was necessary to have a work by Frankenthaler in the exhibition. In searching with the gallery, we discovered that Frank Stella, one of the artists represented by the gallery, had a woodcut edition in his collection: *Radius,* from 1993 (which was later included in the Frankenthaler exhibition at Dulwich Picture Gallery in two versions). Upon first viewing *Radius,* I realised that it would be key to my exhibition.

The Mechanics of Fluids (2018) included artists who give priority to the visualisation of material *on the move*. In fact, in putting the exhibition together, what became evident was not only an interest throughout many of the artists' practices in the motifs or imagery of liquidity, but that this liquidity was embodied in many of the practices and histories of the artists shown: a refusal to become solid in one medium, in one style, in one place.

In the hanging, I realised that the liquid nature of the works did not lie simply in the physical medium of the artist: the colour pours of Lynda Benglis, the bubbling surfaces of Josephine Pryde's photographs, the modular sculptures of Charlotte Posenenske: yes, these works enact a liquidity, but, like in the Frankenthaler print, it was the *movement* between the act (pouring, layering, assembling) and the material *translation* of each artist's gestures where the real "liquid" nature of their work was enacted. The liquid nature of a Lynda Benglis pour piece is not the fact that it was poured, or that it looks liquid: the liquid nature of a Lynda Benglis pour piece is that, as shown in the photographs of her making the work in 1969 (which were taken in the same year as the portraits of Frankenthaler by Ernst Haas), the work exists in the *transition between* a performance moment and a sculptural "document". The means make the ends, because all material transformation is a performance in this world of an abstraction where your body cannot be ignored.

In my broader research into liquidity and gesture, I have found a number of female artists' first-person writing describing themselves, their gestures and themselves as "in between"; and I have followed this logic as a beacon to explore what this desire to be "between" is about.

3   "The CIA not only helped finance MoMA's international exhibitions, it made cultural forays across Europe. In 1950, the Agency created the Congress for Cultural Freedom (CCF), headquartered in Paris. Though it appeared to be an "autonomous association of artists, musicians and writers," it was in fact a CIA funded project to "propagate the virtues of western democratic culture", https://daily.jstor.org/was-modern-art-really-a-cia-psy-op/.

4   America declared war on Germany three days before the submission day of the Society's open call in 1917.

Laura Owens: And most importantly FOR ME at this moment and in my thinking, it is BETWEEN these spaces, the physical spaces, the object and the space of discourse.
BOTH
BETWEEN.[5]

Charlene von Heyl: I build up the shape by destroying it and by laying another shape over it. By building the painting in overlapping layers I would get shapes that I could never have invented. That's what I wanted. There was an early desire to create an alternative mind-space in a painting. It turned out to be something that was nicely situated between the worlds.[6]

Amy Sillman: All I'm really interested in is this quivering moment where something changes into something else in the studio. Changing things completely. I'm looking for a painting that expresses the before and after of itself all in the same frame. I guess it's almost like something that cubists or futurists were trying for. A kind of shattered expression of time and existence? I always think about motion and worry about endings.[7]

In this history of "not one or the other-ness" in women's abstraction, I think it is interesting to point out how Frankenthaler is a strong reference point. She was always central, but between. She was between the group of New York School Expressionist painters such as Lee Krasner and Grace Hartigan and post-painterly colour-field artists. She was between generations of women artists, between the socialist activism of many of her peers who were active members of the Works Progress Administration in the 1930s, and later feminist strategies of the mid-1960s onwards such as those of Carolee Schneemann whose performances emerged from a reaction to "action painting".[8]

I want to discuss abstraction made by women artists in terms of criteria, decisions and rules – rules that perhaps have to be broken or ignored in order to create a new language in painting. What are the criteria to which the "in-between" abstract painters (Frankenthaler, Mary Heilmann, Jo Baer and others) have been subject, what rules have they broken, and what decisions have been made to keep their gestures marginal?

For many women painters, notions of authorship confound the language through which we approach medium as speech. Because there are no embodied tropes (sad, tragic or angry "dude", romantic "intellectual", funny "comedian", cultured "dandy", mad "sage" or "shaman") through which to view our gestures, they are often read as silent or floating alone. Until recently, in much discourse on contemporary women painters, terms such as "unknowability" (Helen Molesworth) and "unquantifiability" (curator and writer Mark Godfrey) prevail:

This lineage raises the question of whether we can locate a feminist position in this approach to abstraction. Molesworth, for one, has already pushed for the term unknowability ... "For me, feminism is a critique of power and mastery, and most of all it's a warning about how the combination of mastery and power has, historically, led to violence. One result of this questioning of power is that unknowability emerges as a kind of virtue."[9]

As a painter, I imagine gesture as something that is liquid and has agency unto itself. At the basis of my interest in this is the question of how to read gestures that have not been animated by history.

5 Laura Owens, 'Picabia', in *Laura Owens*, 626 (New Haven: Yale University Press, 2018), 626.

6 Charlene von Heyl interviewed by Robert Enright and Meeka Walsh 2014: https://bordercrossingsmag.com/article/too-little-and-too-much-all-the-time/. Last accessed 14 July 2023.

7 Interview with Melissa Gordon in *Girls Like Us*, Issue #12, Biography, 2019: 113.

8 "Schneemann developed her approach to making art in dialogue with action painting, a technique pioneered by Jackson Pollock, in which he flung, dripped, and poured paint onto the canvas in dramatic, expressive physical gestures. Fed by feminist thinking of the 1960s and 1970s, she highlighted her own physical experience and point of view in her art", https://www.moma.org/artists/7712.

9 Godfrey, "Statement of Intent", 299.

The theorist Giorgio Agamben begins his essay "Notes on Gesture" (1992) by describing how, in 1886, the scientist Giles de la Tourette "prophesised" or imagined cinematography in his experiment to try to materially visualise a human gait:

> *An approximately seven or eight-meter-long and fifty-centimeter-wide roll of white wallpaper was nailed to the ground and then divided in half lengthwise by a pencil-drawn line. The soles of the experiment's subject were then smeared with iron sesquioxide powder, which stained them with a nice red rust color. The footprints that the patient left while walking along the dividing line allowed a perfect measurement of the gait according to various parameters.[10]*

When I first read this quote, it brought to mind Robert Rauschenberg's Automobile Tire Print from 1953, in which he famously asked John Cage to drive his Model A Ford over some ink and then sheets of A4 paper laid on the ground.

> This question of the *visualisation* in cinematography of the human gesture that Agamben speaks about is the starting point of my enquiry into gesture, as something that behaves within a space or context, of not just painting, but a visual field. What is the "field" of painting?

> *[Leo] Steinberg described Rauschenberg's typical picture surface as "dump, reservoir, switching center". Kraus also characterises Rauschenberg's art in terms of place: discussing the "equal density" which disparate images acquire in [the painting] Small Rebus, she is "struck by the fact that the surface of this painting is a place, a locale, where this kind of equalisation can happen."[11]*

> Implicit in this understanding of the "locale" of a painting is the idea of a venue, a place where something happens: what do gestures enact in this space, and how also, importantly, does the understanding of these "enactments" historically form into a kind of art-historical shape?

The implications of the soak-stain method of painting that Frankenthaler initiated in the early 1950s are particularly interesting because I would argue that her work is the first to intentionally visualise the context of making as an extension of a performance – and in doing so, lays the ground for both "flatbed" works that endeavour to keep the painting surface in the understood realm of the floor or table (to not imagine composition as a driving force) and the "formless" (informe) process that is described by Yve-Alain Bois and Rosalind Krauss as a place where someone has enacted a process of transformation visualised on a painting surface:

> *"The informe would thus specify a certain power that forms have to deform themselves constantly, to pass quickly from the like to the unlike." Didi-Huberman writes."[12]*

To make a distinction, I think of the story of how Pollock, the first to employ the ground as a "field" of action in painting, was psychologically broken by the "performance" that he enacted for the film of Hans Namuth, pretending to make a painting on a sheet of glass as Namuth filmed underneath. Exploding in anger at the end of filming on Thanksgiving Day of 1950, Pollock broke his supposedly two-year sober period, and some might argue descended towards his self-destructive and untimely death. The performance "killed" him because he did not intend the audience to see the shaman like-quality that he describes in the making of his work, or even be aware of his body. The transformative action in his painting was in communion with the surface, whereas I think Frankenthaler was aware of her actions and performance as part of the

10 Giorgio Agamben, "Notes on Gesture", in *Means without End: Notes on Politics*, trans. V. Binetti and C. Casarino (Minneapolis and London: University of Minneapolis Press, [1992] 2000), 2.

11 Craig Owen, "The Allegorical Impulse: Toward a Theory of Postmodernism, Part 2", in *Beyond Recognition: Representation, Power, and Culture*, eds. S. Bryson, B. Kruger, L. Tillamn and J. Weinstock (Berkeley: University of California Press, [1980] 1994), 70-87.

12 Yve-Alain Bois and Rosalind Krauss, *Formless, A User's Guide* (New York: Zone Books, 1997), 80.

understanding of the gestures of her paintings. It was a body (and maybe a character, or a negative space of a character?) that set the material and formed into motion in her work.

> In my own large-scale paintings with many layers, and the painterly installation designs that I employ to hang them on, I am aware of this sense of the animation of space by an active participant arranging, dropping, cutting. I do think of it as distinct from authored gestures, in that, like in Frankenthaler's works, there is an acknowledgment of a performance that has happened "behind" the painting.

What is the language of liquid gestures that so clearly has its genesis in Frankenthaler's work?

> I look to notions of the "flat plane", which is described so well in the following extract from a letter written by painter Jo Baer to artist Bob Morris in 1967 in response to a piece of Morris' writing:

> *Marks on a flat surface are exactly that: marks on a flat surface ... Space illusions are from the Renaissance, where their painted distances carried subliminal teleology ... A painting is an object which has an emphatic frontal surface ... [In my paintings every] part is painted and contiguous to its neighbor: no part is above or below any other part ... There is no illusion. There is no space or interval (time).[13]*

Frankenthaler famously said about her first encounter with Pollock's paintings (and technique) in 1950:

> *"It was as if I suddenly went to a foreign country but didn't know the language, but had read enough and had a passionate interest, and was eager to live there. I wanted to live in this land; I had to live there, and master the language."[14]*

She walked into that world, that painting space, and turned it into a field (without illusion).

//

> In my own body of ongoing paintings titled *Female Readymades*, which were shown in the solo exhibition *Liquid Gestures* at Towner Gallery, Eastbourne, in 2021-22, amongst other spaces since 2018, I want to bring a sense of hanging onto the canvas, and the notion that gestures are "hung on" a painting. I also want to convey a sense of gravity, and a scale that shows a human space or site at which this activity of hanging is taking place. I'm turning the axis of the field of Frankenthaler, but there's still a lot of spilling taking place.
>
>   Things in my paintings oscillate between a real and a represented gravity: ropes, LCD screens, scans of paint on photo paper on aluminium, hooks and handles are all real. A hole is cut out and a sleeve hangs through it. Bags, saws, scarves, rope and chains are exposed directly to silkscreen, like photograms, and printed life size. Paintings are hung on paintings. Paintings are made on paintings. Cut-outs of financial terms that relate to the body – exhaust price, burn rate – are hung with digital drawings of intestines and thick paint.

13   Jo Baer, "Letter to Robert Morris, 1967", in *Broadsides & Belles Lettres, Selected Writings and Interviews 1965–2010*, ed. R. Arkesteijn (Amsterdam: Roma Publications, [1967], 2010), 41.
14   Barbara Rose, *Frankenthaler* (New York: Abrams, 1972), 29.

I paint in a continuous stream of thought. I am working in the liminal space where fields of information and the imaginary field of painting gestures merge.

Who gets to be abstract? What support do I have to engender as an artist, for myself, in order to do this? What language describes what I do when so much of what I do doesn't come into clear contact with histories of painting, because it is multiple, unstructured and gooey?

There are two images of the original *Fountain*. The first was photographed by artist Alfred Steiglitz, on a plinth, in front of a painting in a back room of the Society of Independent Artists in 1917. The second image is a photograph taken on a time-release by Marcel Duchamp, of himself, in his studio, sitting cross legged, under a doorway where he has hung *Fountain*. He has also hung *In Advance of a Broken Arm* and *Bottlerack*. The image is dated 1917. In the book where I found this image, it states that Duchamp spoke of *Fountain* as "Une Femelle Pendue".[15] A hung female form. Gravity suspending something that cannot be abstract.

Une femelle pendue to me is violent, and coy. The gestures of women in early modernism were accumulated by men: the readymade, the "all over" drip gesture of Pollock, many other gestures considered "original" are in fact copies of others – others who were not supported, in the sense of not being elevated by language: it's our job to make sure they aren't hung out to dry.

15 William A. Camfield, *Marcel Duchamp, Fountain* (Houston: The Menil Collection / Houston Fine Art Press, 1989), 23.

the best cure
for lonliness is
solitude.
— Marianne Moore

april 1953

MON	TUE	WED	THU	FRI	SAT
		1	2	3	4
6	7	8	9	10	11
13	14	15	16	17	18
20	21	22	23	24	25
27	28	29	30		

Con Jobs and Exhaustion

(Originally performed at the closing event of WINONA, Brussels, 15 April 2023, announced as *Female Genius Nightclub*. The text was delivered in the mode of a stand-up comedy routine.)

(Intro Song: Schizophrenia (1993) by Sonic Youth, plays out to silence)

In an essay I wrote on heartburn and luxury in art production, titled "Luxury Goods: A Burning Desire", in 2016, I wrote:

The confidence man is a traditional American character, a product of the geography of a new, unregulated country: he is a travelling salesman who arrives to sell what in the end turns out to be lies.

> *But the con man is not a simple thief. He is a pedlar of a concrete good: belief. In fact, from a good con, all you might get is the feeling of being swept along in the fiction of the moment: belief in what turn out to be lies, which feel good at the time. You've lost something, but you still have the fantasy.*

/////

23:22 Sat, 21 Jan 2023 text to A

OK I think I understand my fascination with the con now. There's an increase in financial fraud because it's embedded in our form of contemporary capitalism. And art is the aesthetic of that capital form … I think we're all busy basically participating in a big-ass-con-job.

(Loudly):

**Busy ness! Heh
Busy-ness! No?!**

(Smiling broadly, speaking fast):

busy ness busyness busyness busy-ness, busyness, busyness, business, business business business, Bussinass, bus-nass-nasty, nasty, nasty business.

Part I: The Snow Job: You have to want it

To quote David Hammons:

> *"As an artist I'm not aligned with the collectors or the dealers or the museums; I see them all as frauds."* [1]

What's the business of busy-ness? What systems do I find myself circling in, what activities have I been roped into, what words am I unwilling to speak? Why is everyone saying email is killing them? I heard George Soros at Davos say that email is dead; it's just WhatsApp group chat, cold call, short-attention-shorting it.

> *So busy.* I'm imagining the speed of different fabrics stretched over different bodies, actions documented to near infinity on YouTube emulating the aesthetic vantage point of Jane Fonda, who gave up on politics to *get busy*, counting time away in productive sections of 10, 9, 8 …

1   David Hammons as quoted in Elena Filipovic, *Bliz-aard Ball* Sale (London: Afterall Books, 2017), 45.

Speaking of Spandex, it says today in The New York Times that the ads for crypto-currency at the Superbowl were suspiciously missing. What were those guys busy with?

A sent me an article about the disgraced entrepreneur Charlie Javice after an exchange which included:

20:30 Fri, 20 Jan

      `Not every field rewards directly exploitative and/or self-abusive/`
      `destructive behavior. The arts do. Porn does. Maybe athletics do.`
                                       `Entertainment. And fashion.`

Javice is a woman in her late twenties who sold a completely fabricated start-up company to JP Morgan Chase for 175 million dollars.

(Loud Italian American accent):

> *"We all understand the art of the sale, but some of the things that were being said were just inexcusably inaccurate!"*[2]

What's this grey area of truth in the world of speculation?

Cady Noland begins her 1989 essay "Towards a Metalanguage of Evil," by stating that there is a "meta-game available for use in the United States. The rules of the game, or even that there is a game at all, are hidden to some."[3] The essay goes on to describe in an oblique manner a relationship between X and Y, in which X is constantly, in a Tom-and-Jerry-like scenario, trying to "con" Y.

> *The game is a machine composed of interconnected mechanistic devices ... A con or a snow job is the site at which X preys upon the hopes, fears, and anxieties of Y for ulterior motives and/or personal gain ... These machinations exist a priori of X or Y as an indifferent set of tools and could conceivably be picked up by anyone and used against anyone else.* [4]

Noland's interest in the con is never clearly stated: instead, it is used as a cipher through which to view interactions: personal, political, financial, aesthetic.

The contemporary obsession with the con, arising 35 years after Noland's essay, is evident from a quick scroll of Netflix documentaries: dramas and semi-fictionalised films trace every move of sociopathic behavior: "characters" such as Bernie Madoff, Anna Sorkin, Elizabeth Holms and Theranos and titles like *The Tinder Swindler* (2022), *The Puppet Master* (2022) and *The Great Art Heist* (2021).

"Where did all the money go?", Netflix editors ask over and over again. And we watch: yachts, Michelin restaurants, private clubs, watches, yawn, hotels, beach holidays, gold, yawn, gas, sex, food uneaten on porcelain plates, bodies getting paid to service others.

> These documentaries remind me of watching TV toy store shopping spree competitions as a child during the 1980s, where winning children had 30 seconds to run wild in a fully stocked toy store with an empty shopping trolley. I would watch incredulously as mini-brand obsessives searched the aisles for specific G.I. Joes or Lego, running out of time and grasping in the last seconds for some pathetic bit of plastic.

Which was fabricated just before the train derailed, spilling vinyl chloride all over the place, slowing PVC production down by... absolutely nothing.

2   https://www.forbes.com/sites/alexandralevine/2023/01/19/charlie-javice-jp-morgan-frank-lawsuit/. Last accessed 6 July 2023.

3   Noland, "Towards a Metalanguage of Evil", 410.

4   Ibid.

//

The profit made is always more important than the process of making, in capitalism.

In all ponzi schemes, the con is enacted by taking someone's trustfully given "investment", then gambling or investing it, and re-distributing the winnings or losses in an outline of a pyramid. To keep the money coming in and collapse at bay, the new investors' cash is fed up to the small amount of original investors or the original con artist. Some money is spent, but the con artist, to keep the con going, needs to play with the money, and hide their losses in order to appear "flush", because they know the investment is not sound in the first place.

Incredibly, in the largest known ponzi scheme in history, run by the disgraced banker Bernie Madoff,[5] no one worked with or invested a penny of investors' money. It was simply redistributed, moved around, whilst all the energy was spent on fabricating a fictional space of exclusivity and desire to lure new money.

BZZZZZZZZZZZ TIME'S UP!!!!!!!!

(Bossy voice)

It's all about quality, a male painter tells me. And he's right, it's all about the quality of the surfaces produced: and why not? *So many to choose from.*

Noland also aptly said, a couple of years before *American Psycho* (1991) by Bret Easton Ellis was published:

"The psychopath shares the societally sanctioned characteristics of the entrepreneurial male."[6]

I walked through a Swiss museum recently and had a vision where all the oil paint was like sagging patches of skin, falling off the small squares of rotting linen. Everything from before 1959 screaming PTSD: cuts, holes of colour, blood, shit, lumpen shapes, men holding their passports up to the mirror, misshapen faces.

The thousands of colours in our world now are so sharp! More quality! People are so brightly lit, tight, *flat*.

As I stare at the photo of *Bliz-aard Ball Sale* of David Hammons' work from 1989, in which he sold snowballs at the New York's Cooper Square flea market, I realise that the careful placement of 20 large snowballs, under which are six sets of six snowballs of descending size, looks just like a pyramid.

Part II: The Con Job: You have to believe it

Marcel Duchamp's playing with value as a conceptual mind-fuck with art objects is well-documented, but less so is the idea of Duchamp as a con man. He *is* the perfect confidence-man: convincing people to invest in a completely fictional situation, turning it into profit for his legacy. Duchamp's one and only solo exhibition, in Pasadena in 1963[7] (which Hammons saw) was held during the advent of conceptual strategies in art. Before 1963, when Duchamp finally claimed authorship of the supposedly "original" conceptual artwork *Fountain*, most of the people who knew anything about the original authorship

5   https://www.nytimes.com/2021/04/14/business/bernie-madoff-dead.html.
6   Noland, "Towards a Metalanguage of Evil", 412.
7   Marcel Duchamp, 8 October – 3 November 1963, Pasadena Museum of Art, Pasedena CA, USA.

of *Fountain* were dead (it was only replicated in 1964). Until then, Duchamp was mainly known as the ex-painter and chess-playing curator of Surrealist exhibitions.

> What did Rrose Sélavy make? She made *Air de Paris* (1919). She made *Freshly Painted Widow* (1920). She made *Why Not Sneeze Rose Sélavy?* (1921). Was she the author of *Fountain* from 1917 also? Did she arise out of the fiction created in order to orchestrate an aggressive take over? When absurdity is mixed with intention, even experts can be put off the track.

The profit made is always more important than the process of making (or effects), in capitalism.

//

My parents live in a tiny town in rural Tennessee called Jonesborough. Their town hosts the International Storytelling Festival each year, and thousands of people from around the world come to sit in rocking chairs and listen to people "spin" tales and mirror the way their politicians lie to them.

Some of the audience members probably listen to Salem Radio, which is a national syndicate in America that produces right-wing content for local radio stations. One in five Americans listens to Salem Radio content. In the final episode of an *NPR* special that I listened to recently, Katie Thornton interviews Phil Boyce, the vice president of Salem Radio.[8] She questions him about the radio hosts who knowingly spread misinformation and lies about the 2020 election "theft". She asks if any proof has been found of election fraud, and Boyce explains how his radio hosts are telling the truth, because despite not having proof of election fraud, they *believe* fraud has occurred. And their belief is good enough to report on (for profit).

Narratives – they are spun, bought, dominated...

Or, maybe
(Loudly):

> *"We all understand the art of the sale, but some of the things that are being said are just inexcusably inaccurate!"* [9]

Part III: What you can't do without it

> I'm just so exhausted. I'm going to be honest: having to work full time is exhausting when you have an entire career you are supporting on the side.
> Oh man, the stories of Chris Kraus and Cookie Mueller: girls, you put me off fast money and here I am, trying to operate as a respectable character in an increasingly criminal enterprise.
> Being an artist implies and necessitates having free time, right? But increasingly I find myself surrounded by some deep café culture, itinerant work, grant application writing, MacBook-strapped cultural practices.

Paintings on budget canvases of internet research?
Living with less in order to have more Instagram exposure?

> How can I continue to operate in a world in which the spectrum of support creates increasingly uneven conditions for making work? When children of wealthy industrialists and citizens of countries with vast earth-killing support structures want their subjectivities to be not just *seen,* but

8   The Divided Dial, Episode 5, 15 December 2022: https://www.wnycstudios.org/podcasts/otm/episodes/divided-dial-episode-5-. Last accessed July 5, 2023.

9   https://www.forbes.com/sites/alexandralevine/2023/01/19/charlie-javice-jp-morgan-frank-lawsuit/. Last accessed 6 July 2023.

understood, when collectors' eyes light up realising they *could put their drink on that,* when I look around and realise, in 2023, as Hammons said about the 1980s in New York,

"everybody was just groveling ... anything to be in the room with some money."[10]

Well, the party's over, or maybe it will be on again tomorrow, but somewhere else.

As large gallery rosters swell, becoming the wholesale outlets of institutionally backed art, I feel more and more crushed under the weight of the feeling that I've been conned.

Are leisure and perseverance hegemonic? Am I hanging onto a fantasy?

No one cares. No one's replying to my emails anymore anyway – Didn't you hear? Sorry, we're all outside Trump tower today, we're in the tent, I can't pick up, I'm on the plane.

Busy ness business.

But:::

IT is YOUR choice: YOU, be YOU. This is what we're doing, right? Being ourselves?

I mean, who do you want to be: *The Gentlewoman* cover presentation of a female artist: iPhone in hand, hair smooth from expensive conditioner? Business.

Or, as my ex-gallerist said to me:
"You're not the kind of artist who's ever going to be in *Vogue*."
(Raises eyebrows)

OR: The wife of ..., the nobody, the forgotten genius! The funny old lady, ha ha they are so cute! Like cats!
(Laugh uncontrollably, then stop).

That veil falls as we follow Helen Molesworth in her 2022 podcast *Death of An Artist* to the door of Carle Andre's superior upper west side loft. The doorman repels her politely.

The profit made is always more important than the process of making (or of cleaning up), in capitalism.

All the mess to clean up. Who is cleaning it up? Did Carl Andre clean it up?

//

Recently someone was shocked when I told them I'm only interested in negative comments on my work. "That's so sad", she said. No, sadness has nothing to do with it: I'm interested in negativity because it reveals readings that I am blind to.

Only in the art world do two extreme forms of capital production, with their own forms of exploitation – as A pointed out – come into regular contact: craft and investment.

10   David Hammons as quoted in
    Bliz-aard Ball Sale, 43.

91

//

As I'm hanging work in the collective space of my residency, a "famous artist", to be known hereupon in as FA, is holding his Zoom conference in the high-ceilinged gallery space, rather than in the small, cramped huts where we live. Assurances are given, benches are inquired about, I hear murmurs of "the space looks amazing" and in short, I feel like I'm listening to a sales pitch, until the conversation turns practical: "Everyone's bought these bonds, and then, you know, the value of everyone's bonds goes down when interest rates go up, because, you know, the bonds are literally worth less, so that's what's happening."

> Meanwhile, I'm silk-screening – a backbreaking, 12 hours a day, labour-intensive, thankless, bad-for-my health medium. And FA tells me that the problem with it is that everything done with silkscreen looks so '60s, as he shows me the UV printer that he hires for a cool five hundred a day.

I gotta know what a five dollar shake tastes like.

As Ursula Le Guin quotes the civil rights activist Lillian Smith as saying:

> *"What Freud mistook for her lack of civilisation is woman's lack of loyalty to civilisation."*[11]

> And we can take that a step further, right? It's not just women, it's anyone who's not winning that is uncivilised, don't you think? Or, to put it in other terms: why, if you're excluded from a form of participation, should you give a damn about the game? And let's think about craft-making for a second: in what other world than the art world does someone or a group of people produce a lot of stuff, let's say organic taco shells – why not? – while only one person in one hundred can actually make a living off the black corn organic taco shells, and that one person keeps it all for themselves, while being surrounded by starving taco-shell makers?

It's cool. I went to college with those guys at Zwiner or wherever...

But ... How much better are the tacos?

Part IV: How *you* make value

Nope.

Art has always reflected aesthetically, in a broad and functional sense, the mode of contemporary capital in which it finds itself. Art is bloated, investment heavy, fabricated. Financial bloopers come and go, shuffling investment in an endless shock doctrine, fracking to squeeze every last bit of already accumulated resources. But on a larger scale, art is mirroring itself on a breed of capitalism in which con jobs are rife, because money changes hands over snow jobs. There's coffee, and then there's coffee that's shit out by a small animal, and the person selling that coffee is a much better storyteller.

> I am a female artist, so I must speak twice, and my speech is confusing.

11 Ursula Le Guin, *The Carrier Bag of Fiction* (Peru: Terra Ignota, 2020), 30.

In an essay I wrote in 2015 titled "Presence and Absence" on dropping out, I said:

Increasingly as an artist I have begun to feel my voice becoming disembodied from myself. Who is it that is "speaking"? It is strange to envision oneself as a construct, a concept, outside of one's own body, but that is exactly what is perceived by others: an accumulation of objects, made by a non-entity with a vague persona, skewed and squared by gestures and contexts.

> Dropping out is a gesture of walking out. A strike. A Human Strike. Dropouts walk off the edge of the world in which they exist at the time: off the map, off the grid. As characters for others to see, dropouts act outside the bounds of the playing field of contemporary art, and by doing so, reveal the shape-form of the container: when the boundaries that hold these gestures become immaterial.

//

So can we think of our field as a dumping ground? For ego?

//

(Spoken excitedly!)

> *The team at Studio Olafur Eliasson consists of about ninety people, from craftsmen and specialised technicians, to architects, archivists and art historians, web and graphic designers, filmmakers, cooks, and administrators. They work with Eliasson to develop, produce, and install artworks, projects, and exhibitions, as well as on experimentation, archiving, research, publishing, and communications. In addition to realising artworks in-house, Eliasson and the studio work with structural engineers and other specialists and collaborate worldwide with cultural practitioners, policymakers, and scientists. The studio hosts workshops and events in order to further artistic and intellectual exchanges with people and institutions outside the art world[!]* [12]

//

I'm a failure. No, I am. You might laugh or not think so, it's ok. I've just actually realised this.

Someone I loved dearly passed away suddenly recently. They were a complete dropout. They had no job, they had no money, no home. They refused to participate in any system. They refused not to be alive each day. Until they weren't anymore.

I've realised that if I don't start living without the expectations of success, I'm going to be a failure in so many other ways.

//

12 Olafur Eliasson, "About Studio Olafur Eliasson", https://olafureliasson. net/studio. Last accessed 10 November 2019.

A asked me to clarify, when we spoke last week, after she read this. What am I missing, what have I been cheated of? I answer: no, it's not me, this isn't about me.

I've created the life I want to live, I know exactly what I'm doing.
It's the world I find myself living in that's being cheated:

Believing

That value itself

Makes anything worth living for.

/////////////

(Brightening right up, typical stand-up intro):

So! One night, in my mid-30s, at an opening, I was talking to an artist who I
barely knew at all, about the endless slog of my teaching job at Goldsmiths
with newborn twins.

"How did *you* get that job?" He asked.

[Suppressed laughter in the crowd]

"Well," I said,

"Because I'm a fucking genius."

(Cue to: Not the End of The World (2020) by Katy Perry)

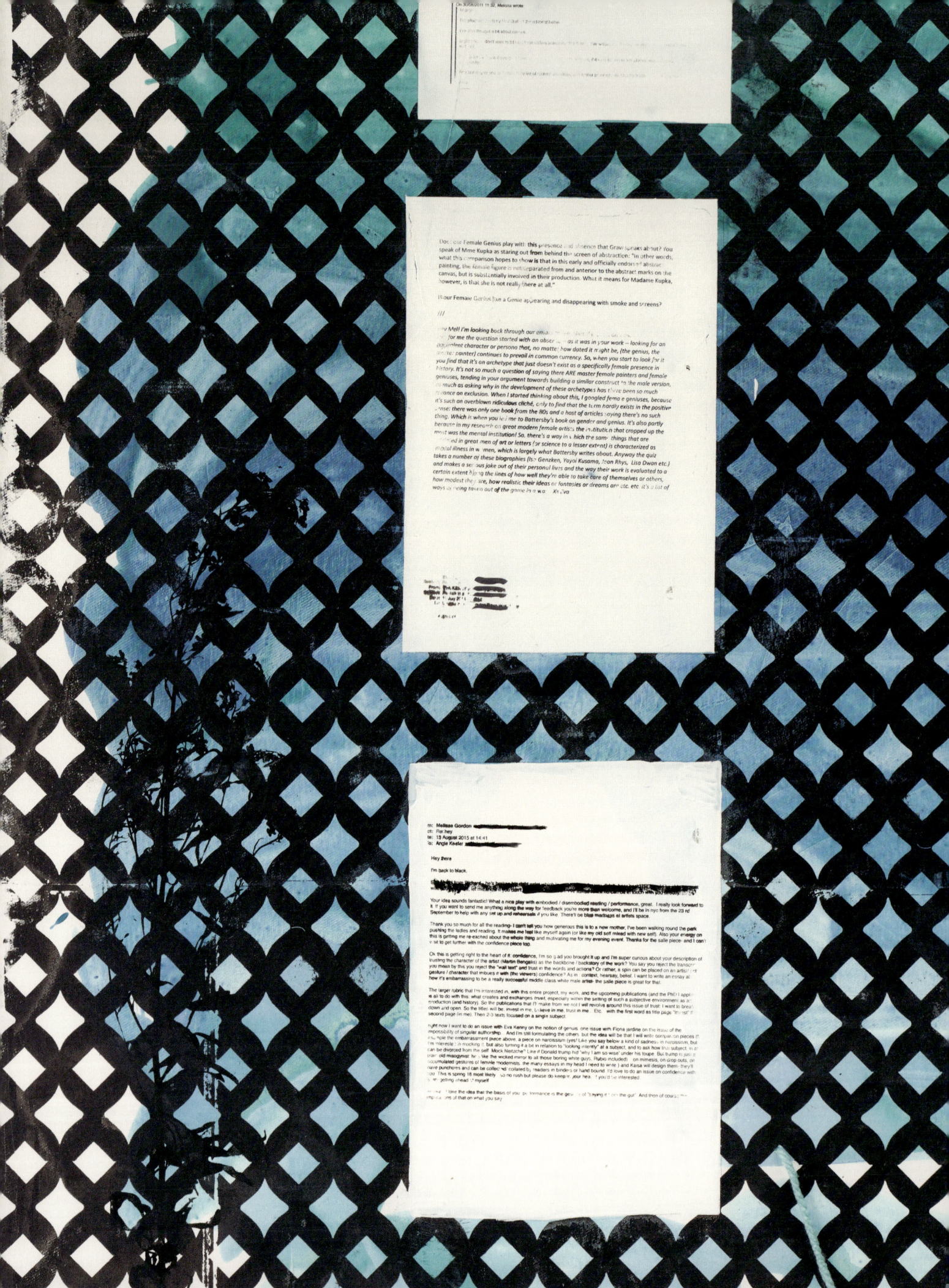

Does our Female Genius play with this presence and absence that Gravel speaks about? You speak of Mme Kupka as staring out from behind the screen of abstraction: "In other words, what this comparison hopes to show is that in this early and officially endorsed abstract painting, the female figure is not separated from and anterior to the abstract marks on the canvas, but is substantially involved in their production. What it means for Madame Kupka, however, is that she is not really there at all."

Is our Female Genius like a Genie appearing and disappearing with smoke and screens?

///

Hey Mell I'm looking back through our emails . . .
. . . for me the question started with an obser . . . as it was in your work – looking for an argument character or persona that, no matter how dated it might be, (the genius, the master painter) continues to prevail in common currency. So, when you start to look for it you find that it's an archetype that just doesn't exist as a specifically female presence in history. It's not so much a question of saying there ARE master female painters and female geniuses, tending in your argument towards building a similar construct to the male version, as much as asking why in the development of THESE archetypes has there been so much insistence on exclusion. When I started thinking about this, I googled fema e geniuses, because it's such an overblown ridiculous cliché, only to find that the term hardly exists in the positive sense: there was only one book from the 80s and a host of articles saying there's no such thing. Which is when you le . me to Battersby's book on gender and genius. It's also partly because in my research on great modern female artists, the institution that cropped up the most was the mental institution! So, there's a way in v hich the same things that are praised in great men of art or letters (or science to a lesser extent) is characterized as mental illness in w men, which is largely what Battersby writes about. Anyway the quiz takes a number of these biographies (i.e. Genzken, Yayoi Kusama, Jean Rhys, Lisa Owan etc.) and makes a serious joke out of their personal lives and the way their work is evaluated to a certain extent along the lines of how well they're able to take care of themselves or others, how modest they are, how realistic their ideas or fantasies or dreams are etc. etc. it's a list of ways of being taken out of the game in a wa . . . Xx va

---

Hey there

I'm back to black.

Your idea sounds fantastic! What a nice play with embodied / disembodied reading / performance, great. I really look forward to it. If you want to send me anything along the way for feedback you're more than welcome, and I'll be in nyc from the 23 rd September to help with any set up and rehearsals if you like. There's be blue madness at artists space.

Thank you so much for all the reading- I can't tell you how generous this is to a new mother. I've been walking round the park pushing the ladies and reading. It makes me feel like myself again (or like my old self mixed with new self). Also your energy on this is getting me re-excited about the whole thing and motivating me for my evening event. Thanks for the salle piece- and I can't wait to get further with the confidence piece too.

Oh this is getting right to the heart of it: confidence, I'm so glad you brought it up and I'm super curious about your description of trusting the character of the artist (Martin Bengalis) as the backbone / backstory of the work? You say you reject the transpo . . . you mean by this you reject the "wall text" and trust in the words and actions? Or rather, a spin can be placed on an artist . . . gesture / character that imbues it with (the viewers) confidence? As in: context, hearsay, belief. I want to write an essay about how it's embarrassing to be a really successful middle class white male artist- the salle piece is great for that.

The larger rubric that I'm interested in, with this entire project, my work, and the upcoming publications (and the PhD I appli . . . as all to do with this: what creates and exchanges trust, especially within the setting of such a subjective environment as an production (and history). So the publications that I'll make from we not I will revolve around this issue of trust. I want to break down and open. So the titles will be: invest in me, believe in me, trust in me. Etc. with the first word as title page "In est" t second page be me). Then 2-3 texts focussed on a single subject.

right now I want to do an issue with Eva Kenny on the notion of genius. one issue with Fiona Jardine on the issue of the impossibility of singular authorship. And I'm still formulating the others, but the idea will be that I will conjure up pieces (I . . . topic (the embarrassment piece above, a piece on narcissism (yes! Like you say below a kind of sadness in narcissism, but the interest is a mocking (. but also turning it a bit in relation to "looking intently" at a subject, and to ask how this subject, in a . . . can be divorced from the self. Mock Nietzche? Like if Donald trump hid "why I am so wise under his tongue. So bump in just t poor old misogynist for . . . like the wicked mirror to all those boring white guys, Rubio included: . on mimesis, on drop outs, on accumulated gestures of female modernists, the many essays in my head I need to write.) and Kasia will design them- they'll have punchers and can be collected/ collated by readers in binders or hand bound. I'd love to do an issue on confidence with you This is spring 16 most likely - so no rush but please do keep in your hea . I'd be interested . . . . . . getting ahead of myself

. . . . I love the idea that the basis of you, be immanence is the gest . . . d of "saying it on the gut." And then of cours . . . . . empirical ones of that on what you say

On Time: Not your Comrade

(A complete re-working of a talk originally delivered as an introduction
to the symposium "Time as Medium" at the Astrup Fearnley Museet in Oslo,
on 2 May 2023.)

We arrive
Fairly fully formed
To this place

No one is waiting
      For any move to be made
Simultaneous-ness, a continual flow of events and thoughts and

Rather, there is something rotten at the core
Of how the movement of all this information
pushes
And pulls, stacks and
washes itself
And the tide pulls out to reveal
What is left.

Because
    (as the hundreds turn to thousands)

Like Wile E. Coyote, I draw a circle on the rock face, paint it in: I watch you walk through it,
And I hit a wall.
Gravity, of material
an endless re-imagining and re-grouping of symbols and stuff.

    **To say someone's work is timeless would perhaps be one of
the more disturbing comments to make.**

Events unfolding in cycles of:
Aesthetics, media, exhibitions, politics, eras, years, a millisecond that is recognised as a
slight pause by the algorithm, the time of refresh.

We must, today, perhaps first accept that we are all outdated, to be human.

    *To be con-temporary does not necessarily mean to be present, to be here-
and-now; it means to be "with time" rather than "in time". "Contemporary" in
German is zeitgenössisch, [and] can thus be understood as being a "comrade
of time" – as collaborating with time, helping time when it has problems.[1]*

    **No, I am not a comrade of time, not it's agent, not it's
friend.**

    No, not the acting, not the material manipulation, not the adding, the
pouring, the cutting, the letting dry, cracking, crumbling, the sanding,
the layering, the masking, not the spatula-ing like cake putty, the scumbling,

1   Boris Groys, "Comrades of
Time", *e-flux Journal*, Issue #11
(December 2009), https://
www.e-flux.com/journal/11/
61345/comrades-of-time/.

the great arm stroke, the letting it spread...
But the looking back. The regret and confusion at the object in progress, the
embarrassment, the good idea turned sour, the peeling back, the reclaiming
and clawing out of something useful, from what, most likely, was uncool,
unfinished and ungainly at one, or all, moments.

Unknowability, in-between-ness, unquantifiability, "not clear" etc.
They're not good enough, to me. They're not the leftovers, they're the conditions.
Try harder.

Suffocated (embarrassed).

But what of us who have a lack of loyalty to "con-temporary" time? What if we're
interested in time's problems from a different relationship to time because we're surfing
a different wave?

Forget the list, the day is done.
And other times? Of seasonal, migratory, the time of sickness, of waiting,
loss, silence, sadness, of inquisitiveness, drifting, of the cacophony of
children laughing, of the radio on low, weather, of things beyond our control
or understanding, of time not to be googled or time sitting in water versus
on land.

Gestures
rather
reverberate, echo, back and forwards
On a journey
Hitting walls of moments,
Being transformed and transforming? (They aren't singular).

Joining a large, ongoing flow, forming and re-forming, layering and accumulating.

Not squeezed through that asshole time.

I'm writing so you can't be confused when I'm not here about context.

Chronos: the modern taskmaster, marching and rewarding,
bestowing gifts upon comrades:
Slaves to progression.

Sorry, I'm leaving you for Kairos, the archer and weaver.
Waiting for the moment to release.
With them I'm seeing the hole through which the arrow will pass,
and the passing of that arrow.

stack all the old hopes on top of each other, watch them get buried
and let,   the waves of what is happening
wash over you

List of Works

All works courtesy of the artist

p. 2
Intestine Painting, 2018
Acrylic and silkscreen on canvas,
95 × 115 cm

p. 5
*Female Readymade (Weeds, correspondence
with Marina and Kaisa about LABOUR
magazine (2011), letters with Eva on
Female Genius (2014), note to Angie on
Confidence (2015), rope, excerpt from Drop
Outs: Slackers, Sociopaths, Social Workers
(2013), cut-out of 'On Friendship' by Celine
Condorelli, PERSONA, 'What's the hook,
What's the handle?' painting for Rita with
hook and flexible arc ruler, ferns, x in yarn),*
2021 (detail)
Acrylic, silkscreen, hook and architect's
ruler on canvas, 180 × 200 cm
Photo: Kristien Daem

p. 6
*Female Readymade Pt.I (Human Capital,
burning car, barricade, Hydrofeminism,
Opel Tometi's hands, dancing, steering
wheel, chain, intestines, tape, rearview
mirror),* 2020
Acrylic, silkscreen, marble dust, flashe
on canvas, 180 × 200 cm
Photo: Aad Hoogendoorn

p. 9
*Female Readymade Pt.II (Intestines, belt,
tape, tope, elephant and hole, voting booth
fabric and sign, licence plate),* 2020
Acrylic, silkscreen, marble dust, flashe
on canvas, 180 × 200 cm
Photo: Aad Hoogendoorn

p. 10
*Female Readymade (Drop Outs, Letter to
Dr. Brunn, chain, dollar bill in homage to
Laurie Parsons, Lee Lozano's Notebook,
ratchet, list of verbs of gestures of dropping
out, large wash, sleeve, medicine, painting),*
2020 (detail)
Acrylic, silkscreen, flashe, marble dust,
dollar bill on canvas, 180 × 200 cm
Photo: Kristien Daem

p. 13
*Female Readymade (Mesh, weeds, two holes,
writing on voice, Iris pouring water on liars
to render them unconscious, eye projecting
light spectrum),* 2022 (detail)
Acrylic, chalk, pigment, silkscreen on
canvas, 115 × 95 cm
Photo: Stephen White and Co.

p. 14
*Female Readymade (Intestines, rope, hole,
wood and erasure),* 2019
Acrylic and silkscreen on canvas,
180 × 200 cm
Photo: Kristien Daem

p. 17
Installation View, "The Mechanics of
Fluids", Marianne Boesky Gallery, New
York
Background: Melissa Gordon
Make a Mess, Clean it up, 2018
Silkscreen on raw canvas, 3,500 × 1,200 cm
Foreground: Charlotte Posenenske
Series D, 1967/2018
Steel, Dimensions variable
Photo: Jason Wysche

p. 18
Installation View, *Something Stronger
Than Me*,* WIELS Centre for
Contemporary Art, Brussels
Background: Melissa Gordon
Make a Mess, Clean it up, 2017
Silkscreen on raw canvas, 3,500 × 1,200 cm
Foreground: Rita McBride
Guide Rail, 2017
Painted Wood, dimensions variable
Extension (Micky Damm, Rita McBride &
Christian Odzuck)
No Title, 2017
Aluminium pallet, tyre rims,
dimensions variable
Photo: Kristien Daem

p. 21
*Female Readymade (Safety mesh, bra,
excerpt about Duchamp's 'Femelle Pendu',
pill packet, bungee cord, cut-out of 'Hon'
(1966), belt, the female superstar index,
painting and rope),* 2021–22 (detail)
Acrylic, pigment, flashe, marble dust,
silkscreen on canvas, 180 × 200 cm
Photo: Peter Tijhuis

p. 22
*Female Readymade (Chains, clock hands,
Etienne Decroux, wires, my hand with
Attie's painting on it),* 2021-22 (detail)
Acrylic, marble dust, Epson photograph
on aluminium, silkscreen, pigment,
180 × 200 cm
Photo: Peter Tijhuis

p. 25
*Female Readymade (Chainlink fence, string,
paintbrush, jeans and weeds),* 2021 (detail)
Acrylic, pigment, flashe, marble dust,
silkscreen, on raw canvas, 95 × 115 cm
Photo: Peter Tijhuis

p. 26
Installation view, *Liquid Gestures,*
Towner Gallery, Eastbourne
*Female Readymade (Rope, belt, Attie's
drawing, wood shape, intestine, lingerie,
painting),* 2019
Acrylic, silkscreen, flashe and painting on
raw fabric (50 × 50 cm) on canvas,
180 × 200 cm
Photo: Rob Harris

p. 89
Female Readymade (X-ray of Mondrian painting, sticks from Marlow Moss paintings, re-painting of The Sea of Ice, *George Sand, house on the dutch dunes, boots,* The Waves, *riding crop, bungee cord, wind vane, fishing net, cut out* Fluid Concept, *digital wave erasure)*, 2021 (detail)
Acrylic, flashe, silkscreen on canvas,
180 × 200 cm
Photo: Kristien Daem

p. 90
Myopic View (1929 / 2021), 2023 (detail)
Acrylic, marble dust, pigment and
silkscreen on canvas, 180 × 200 cm
Photo: Kristien Daem

p. 93
Myopic View (1928 / 2019), 2023 (detail)
Acrylic, marble dust, pigment and
silkscreen on canvas, 180 × 200 cm
Photo: Kristien Daem

p. 94
Myopic View (1930 / 2023), 2023 (detail)
Acrylic, marble dust, pigment and
silkscreen on canvas, 180 × 200 cm
Photo: Kristien Daem

p. 97
Female Readymade (Fat Chance, scarf, Material Evidence painting, stud wall),
2018-19 (detail)
Acrylic, silkscreen, marble dust,
180 × 200 cm
Photo: Kristien Daem

p. 98
Female Readymade (Weeds, correspondence with Marina and Kaisa about LABOUR magazine (2011), letters with Eva on Female Genius (2014), note to Angie on Confidence (2015), rope, excerpt from Drop Outs: Slackers, Sociopaths, Social Workers (2013), cut-out of On Friendship *by Celine Condorelli, PERSONA, "What's the hook, What's the handle?" painting for Rita with hook and flexible arc ruler, ferns, x in yarn)*,
2021 (detail)
Acrylic, silkscreen, hook and architect's
ruler on canvas, 180 × 200 cm
Photo: Kristien Daem

p. 101
What is left (Embarrassment), 2023 (detail)
Acrylic, pigment and plastic on canvas,
80 × 100 cm
Photo: Kristien Daem

Afterword

Vital Signs is a compendium of texts produced by Melissa Gordon over a period spanning almost a decade. Writing is not an adjunct to, but is an integral facet of Gordon's work as an artist; the formal and technical properties of paint and screen-printing shape her use of language. Analogous strategies of reproduction, repetition and bricolage are central throughout her work. In texts and paintings alike, Gordon fuses subjective expressions with extant found signs extracted from a multitude of sources. And as the details from her *Female Readymade* series presented in the preceding pages demonstrate, representational details are married with gestural abstraction. Correspondingly, Gordon's writing possesses a dense intertextual quality; personal prose is punctuated by specific passages selected for their capacity to antagonise.

Gordon's paintings and installations can be assessed on their own terms, but viewing them in conjunction with these writings is illuminating and clarifies her position on the visual vocabulary she has cultivated. Consider, for example, how print – which is central to Gordon's output – has historically been a medium inextricably linked to dissent and the dissemination of disputatious ideas. Screen-printing – such an essential component of Gordon's work – also carries a specific set of connotations. Originally used for commercial purposes, it was embraced by a generation of artists who contributed to the deposition of Abstract Expressionism in the 1960s. These writings make clear the lineage of discourse informing Gordon's work and underscore the continued potency of some of the ideas that underpinned second-wave feminism. [1]

The nine pieces of writing in this publication introduce us to a pantheon of polestars that galvanise Gordon's position as an artist. Some of these figures are friends and collaborators; others have become familiar indirectly via their cultural contribution or posthumous legacy. Of particular importance to Gordon's worldview are Cady Noland, Lee Lozano, Charlotte Posenenske and Laurie Parsons. Although dissimilar in their oeuvres, these artists are united by their withdrawal from the artworld and rejection of an apparatus that conflates artist and celebrity. Gordon reflects upon some of the disruptive qualities inherent in these artists' work and also exposes how the historicisation and institutionalisation of an artist often results in (or necessitates) the neutralisation of polemical aspects of their work.

Attention is persistently drawn to structural sexism and Gordon sheds light on some of the barriers, obstacles and hierarchies that shape our cultural landscape whilst also showing how they are built upon increasingly shaky ground. A contention that recurs throughout this book is that the narrative of modernism as we know it is essentially a succession of monolithic creation myths that rely upon the notions of individual (and predominantly male) genius. Gordon shares the observation articulated by Helen Molewesorth that "Genealogies for art made by women aren't so clear, largely because they are structured by a shadowy absence." [2]

Predecessors such as Janet Sobel and Baroness Elsa von Freytag-Loringhoven, whose legacies were unjustly eclipsed or wilfully obscured, are acknowledged in these writings. This particular facet of Gordon's writing chimes with the broader contemporary field of scholarship and curating that seeks to recuperate overlooked talent, particularly that of women who participated in episodes of art-historical significance. While this tendency towards rediscovery undoubtedly has a positive angle, it frequently results in reductive readings of a given artist's legacy. Their marginal status is fetishised and they become known purely for the fact that they were overlooked, while the very aspects of their work that may have made them relevant in the first place are glossed over. Gordon points to this quandary, calling for something greater than mere "acceptance as an end unto itself" and demands that "a change must happen ... their gestures must burst the walls, and as Luce Irigaray implies, go everywhere."

Seven of the nine texts were written specifically to be presented – or in the case of the more recent pieces, performed – live in front of audiences. As a result, they include stage directions and alternating dialogue and therefore read somewhat like a playscript. Although no longer enlivened by those vital ingredients of tone, pitch or gesticulation, their colour presentation here permits differentiation and underscores the polyphonic quality of Gordon's writing. In addition to quotes

1   Some of the issues addressed in these writings resonate with Linda Nochlin's watershed 1971 essay *Why Have There Been No Great Women Artists?*, particularly those pertaining to notions greatness and genius.

from various artists and writers, several of these pieces contain the artist's own disharmonious, occasionally contradictory voices. We hear the author "talking to herself"; an omniscient voice that reports the author's excessively critical (and self-deprecating) self.

While humour runs throughout, it is always tempered by a palpable sense of defiance. Gordon expresses exasperation with an increasingly standardised and conservative cultural landscape in which self-marketing and consistency of product are promulgated. In these pieces, personal experiences, moments with a diaristic quality, converge with something that occasionally resembles reportage. Gordon's most recent writing – like her recent painting – is imbued with details that locate her work specifically in the recent past and present. There are oblique references to the consequences of the 2020 United States presidential election; to Brexit and the toughening of fortress Europe, and to the unclear but undoubtedly long-term repercussions of pandemia.

The increasingly professionalised and neoliberal tenor of contemporary culture encourages artists to cast themselves as individualised agents in competition with one another. Inevitably, this not only results in alienation but also undermines possibilities for solidarity. Gordon's work is of a staunchly idealistic bent and, as the short introductions accompanying each text highlight, she is invested in the social milieux that emerge around art. There is an interest in promoting collegiality; in bringing people together in informal environments; an aspiration to extend beyond the canvas or printed page into the circuitry of human relations. A desire for restitution runs through these writings, some of which occasionally approach a rallying cry, urging us to organise and overthrow hierarchy culture. Ultimately, this book is a testament to the fact that it is incumbent upon all of us to try and create the sort of art world that we want to be part of. To conclude with the words of Lee Lozano, "There are more & more freedoms to be invented by mankind … we have to invent new freedoms." [3]

Pádraic E. Moore, Autumn 2023

2   Helen Molesworth, "How to Install Art as a Feminst", *Women Artists at the Museum of Modern Art*, ed. Cornelia Butler and Alexandra Schwartz (New York: Museum of Modern Art, 2010), 504.

3   Lee Lozano, private notebook (unpublished), no. 7, 120.

Biographies

Melissa Gordon is an American-British artist, writer, teacher, organiser and publisher based in Brussels. She is Professor of Painting at Oslo Art Academy. In her visual work, Gordon utilises a number of tools including silkscreen, text, cuts and collage to arrange surfaces that investigate the material histories of painting. In dialogue with her pictorial practice, Gordon's writing addresses questions of gender and liquidity in relationship to authorship and painterly histories.

Pádraic E. Moore is an Irish curator, writer and art historian.

Artist's Acknowledgements

Thank you to all those who have made space for my voice: Henry Andersen, Devrim Bayer, Manon de Boer, Richard Burkitt, Fulvia Carnevale, Noelle Collins, Maartje Fliervoet, Sophía Hernández Chong Cuy, Maxine Kopsa, Kaisa Lassinaro, Solveig Østebø, Daniel Rother, Daniel Sturgis, Marina Vishmidt;

to those who took the time to read and ask difficult questions: Chris Evans, Angie Keefer, Eva Kenny, Natasha Soobramanien;

to Jessica Wiesner, for the title, and for her ideas on female time;

to Rita McBride for twenty years of iron support;

to Stijn Maes, whose initiative and support has made both this publication and much of my recent work possible;

to Sara De Bondt for her design of this book;

and to Antony Hudek and Pádraic E. Moore for their editorial input.

Colophon

Vital Signs: Writings on Gesture
Melissa Gordon

Text: Melissa Gordon
Afterword: Pádraic E. Moore
Copy editing: Antony Hudek
Proofreading: Melissa Larner
Design: Sara De Bondt
Printing: die Keure
Typefaces: Atlas Grotesk, Faune, Adelphe, Kalice, Sniglet, NotCourierSans, Arial, Yatra One, PicNic, Martina Plantijn

Co-published by

Occasional Papers
occasionalpapers.org
ISBN: 978-1-9196277-2-4

Frans Masereel Centrum
fransmasereelcentrum.be

Cover: *Make a mess, Clean it up*, 2018
Silkscreen on canvas (detail)

All images courtesy the artist and Cosar Gallery, Düsseldorf; Stigter van Doesburg, Amsterdam; Barbara Seiler, Zürich

Occasional Papers